Essential
Budapest

by
CHRISTOPHER AND MELANIE RICE

PASSPORT BOOKS
NTC/Contemporary Publishing Company

Published by Passport Books, an imprint of NTC/Contemporary Publishing Company, 4255 West Touhy Avenue, Lincolnwood (Chicago), Illinois 60646–1975 U.S.A.

The contents of this publication are believed correct at the time of printing. Nevertheless, the publishers cannot accept responsibility for errors or omissions, nor for changes in details given. We are always grateful to readers who let us know of any errors or omissions they come across, and future printings will be updated accordingly.

Published by Passport Books in conjunction with The Automobile Association of Great Britain.

Written by Christopher and Melanie Rice
"Peace and Quiet" section by Paul Sterry

Library of Congress Catalog
Card Number 94–68547
ISBN 0–8442–8902–7

Printed in Trento, Italy

Front cover picture: Dolls in traditional costume

The weather chart displayed on **page 98** of this book is calibrated in °C and millimeters. For conversion to °F and inches simply use the following formula:

$$25 \cdot 4mm = 1 \text{ inch} \qquad °F = 1 \cdot 8 \times °C + 32$$

This book employs a
simple rating system to help
choose which places to visit:

✓   'top ten'

◆◆◆ do not miss

◆◆   see if you can

◆   worth seeing if
     you have time

**Country Distinguishing
Signs**
On the maps, international
distinguishing signs indicate
the location of countries
around Hungary Thus:

Ⓐ = Austria
㏄ = Czech Republic
㋬ = Croatia
㏖ = Romania
㏚ = Slovak Republic
㏒ = Slovenia
㋞ = Ukraine
㋽ = Yugoslavia

STREET NAMES

STREET NAMES
Street names in Budapest have changed.
Some names printed on maps and those
actually seen on streets may not always
tally. The following list of new and old
street names may help visitors find their
way around the city.

New	Old
Aladár u.	Asztalos János u. (I. ker.)
Andrássy út	Népköztársaság útja (VI. ker.)
Apát u.	Bihari Mor u. (III. ker.)
Árpád u.	Hikádé Aladár u. (XIX. ker.)
Arvacska u.	Gajdán Imre u. (III. ker.)
Bácskai u.	Révai József u. (XIV. ker.)
Bagolyvár u.	Antos István u. (XIV. ker.)
Bajnok u.	Bokányi Desző (VI. ker.)
Bank u.	Lengyel Gyula u. (V. ker.)
Emilia u.	Baktai Gyula u. (XIV. ker.)
Erzsébet kőrút	Lenin kőrút (VII. ker.)
Erzsébet tér	Engels tér (V. ker.)
Ferenciek tere	Felszabadulás tér
Fiastyúk u.	Thälmann u. (XIII. ker.)
Fővám tér	Dimitrov tér (V. IX.)
Gömb u.	Kruzslák Béla u. (XIII. ker.)
Gyöngyvirág u.	Ságvári Endre u. (XVIII. ker.)
Haller u.	Hámán Kató u. (IX. ker.)
Hermina út	Május l út (XIV. ker.)
Hofherr Albert u.	Vörös csillag u. (XIX. ker.)
Hold u.	Rosenberg házaspár u. (V. ker.)
Honvéd tér	Néphadsereg tér (V. ker.)
Jávor u.	Szantó Béla u. (XIV. ker.)
Kálváriahegy u.	Merengo u. (XXII. ker.)
Kard u.	Hatvany Lajos u. (I. ker.)
Kerekes u.	Poscher János u. (XIII. ker.)
Király u.	Majakovszkij u. (VI., VII. ker.)
Királoyok útja	Vörös Hadsereg útja (III. ker.)
Kis Korona u.	Magyar Lajos u. (III. ker.)
Lomb u.	Vágó Béla u. (XIII. ker.)
Lónyay u.	Szamuely u. (IX. ker.)
Lovas út	Sziklai Sándor u. (I. ker.)
Miklós u.	Zamercev tér (III. ker.)
Nádor u.	Münnich Ferenc u. (V. ker.)
Násznagy u.	Sollner u. (XIII. ker.)
Oktogon	November 7. tér (VI. ker.)
Pacsirtamező u.	Korvin Ottó u. (III. ker.)
Pannónia u.	Rajk László u. (XIII. ker.)
Podmaniczky u.	Rudos Laszló u. (VI. ker.)

Püspök u.	Ják köz (XXII. ker.)
Rona u.	Lumumba u. (XIV. ker.)
Sas u.	Guszey u. (V. ker.)
Szentharomság tér	Nagytetényi Szolo ter (XXII. ker.)
Szent István tér	Budafoki tér (XXII. ker.)
Szent János u.	Somogyi Miklós u. (III. ker.)
Szent Korona u.	Tegzes u. (XXII. ker.)
Szent László út	Mautner Sándor u. (XIII. ker.)
Szentlélek tér	Korvin Ottó tér (III. ker.)
Szérűskert u.	Darvas József u. (III. ker.)
Teréz Kőrut	Lenin kőrút (VI. ker.)
Thurzó u.	Muck Lajos u. (XIII. ker.)
Tisza u.	Tisza Antal u. (XIII. ker.)
Újpesti rakpart	Kun Béla rakpart (XIII. ker.)
Üllöi út	Vörös Hadsereg útja (XVIII., XIX)
Vajkay u.	László Jenő u. (V. ker.)
Vámház körút	Tolbuhin körút (V., IX. ker.)
Vas Gereben u.	Vörös október u. (XIX. ker.)
Vasút sor	Martos Flóra sétány (III. ker.)
Vértanúk tere	Ságvári tér (V. ker.)
Zoltán u.	Beloiannisz u. (V. ker.)

Times are changing for Hungary, but folk tradition remains strong

INTRODUCTION

Budapest, the capital of Hungary, lies at the very heart of Europe, Buda on the left, or west, bank of the famous River Danube (alas, no longer blue), Pest on the right, or east, bank. A busy, bustling city with more than two million inhabitants (one in every five Hungarians lives in Budapest), Buda and Pest together also make up the political, commercial and industrial hub of the entire country. Hungary, despite its small size (in area only two-thirds that of England), is at the cutting edge of the changes now transforming Central Europe. In April 1990 more than 40 parties contested the first free elections to be held since World War II. The overall winner was József Antall's Democratic Forum – a centre-right grouping espousing capitalist values and a return to a more traditional sense of nationhood (the party's emblem shows the ancient coat of arms breaking through the grey mould of Soviet-imposed Communism). The biggest surprise, however, was the strong showing, especially in Budapest, of the new youth movement known as Fidesz. Predictably, this party has provided Hungary with its youngest MP – Tamás Deutsch, aged only 23.

Recent events in Hungary have been momentous, but its history has ever been chequered: this 1849 print shows peasants in battle array during the War of Independence

Another significant period of Hungary's history was the 25-year regency of Miklós Horthy, seen here riding into Budapest at the head of his counter-revolutionary army in 1919

Budapest has been centre-stage for a number of other remarkable events during the last few years, events full of symbolic significance for Hungarians: the reinterment of the disgraced former premier, Imre Nagy, the erection of a memorial to the victims of the holocaust, the removal of the red star from the Parliament Building, streets reverting to their pre-war names (November 7. tér to Oktogon for example). Budapest has also received a number of distinguished foreign guests recently – even the former heir to the imperial throne, Count Otto von Hapsburg, has visited the country in a symbolic act of reconciliation. 'Renewal' (the Hungarian equivalent of *Perestroika*) is currently transforming the face of commerce and industry. Trade barriers are coming down to facilitate closer ties with the EC countries – Hungary hopes eventually to become a member in its own right. State subsidies are being abolished and state industries sold off, collectivised farming is under review, private housing is already a reality (you can actually buy property through an estate agent in Budapest), the stock exchange has been revived, even credit cards are being

INTRODUCTION

Dressed in a highly decorative herdsman's costume, a zither player entertains tourists in the Fishermen's Bastion

introduced. Most of these changes are welcomed by Hungarians but the side-effects are severe. Inflation is currently running between 20 and 25 per cent, and unemployment is at 12 per cent. People are concerned about housing, the environment, rising crime and other problems. Yet, there is an overriding air of optimism, a confidence in the future.

Budapest is a beautiful city, as you will soon discover for yourself. It is also a fascinating one. There are the sights – Castle Hill, the Fishermen's Bastion, Parliament, Heroes' Square; the faded monuments of bygone eras; the splendid views across the Danube; the pavement cafés, restaurants and nightclubs; the excursions to the Buda Hills, the towns of the Danube Bend and Lake Balaton. You will find shops galore, tree-lined avenues, parks and museums – something for everyone in fact. That is the magic of Budapest. One word of warning, however. The language of the Hungarians (or Magyars, as they call themselves) is unlike any other most visitors will know and guesswork will get you nowhere with deciphering it.

BACKGROUND

There were settlers in the area now made up by Buda and Pest as long ago as 2000 BC and probably much earlier (ornaments and graves have been found on Csepel Island and on both banks of the Danube). In the 6th century BC the Scythians arrived from the northern shores of the Black Sea, and in their wake came a number of Celtic tribes from the area of modern France, including the Eravisci, who inhabited the slopes of Buda's Gellért Hill. The Eravisci were craftsmen, familiar with the potter's wheel; some of their work, coins and jewellery, for example, has survived and may be seen in the Hungarian National Museum. They were later assimilated by the Romans, who had advanced their frontier to the Danube in the 1st century AD. The province of Pannonia (now western Hungary) was divided in two in the following century and Aquincum (now Óbuda) became the capital. Aquincum was basically a garrison town with 6,000–10,000

The view from the roof-tops of Castle Hill, Buda, across the Danube to the Parliament building

soldiers. An amphitheatre was built for their entertainment and its remains can still be seen today near the Árpád Bridge. The Romans also built fortifications on the Pest side of the Danube and the bastion of the fortress known as Contra-Aquincum can be viewed in the centre of Március 15 tér.

The Magyar Conquest

When the imperial forces departed early in the 5th century, Aquincum was occupied for a time by the Huns (medieval chroniclers supposed that Buda was named after Attila's brother). Attila himself died in AD 453 and for several centuries thereafter Hungary was overrun by a succession of barbarian tribes. The Magyars followed the Avars, arriving in 896 from the region between the Volga River and the Ural Mountains, and immediately set out to conquer the entire Carpathian Basin. Their leader, Árpád, is said to have set up camp on Csepel Island, to the south of Budapest. Superb horsemen with a fearsome reputation, their restiveness soon led them to expand westwards in the direction of Bavaria and northern Italy until they were eventually halted in 933. Árpád's grandson, Prince Géza, embarked on a policy of consolidation which entailed the nation's conversion to Christianity (a decision taken purely for reasons of national security). His son, Stephen (István) won official recognition from the pope, who provided the crown for his coronation in December 1000. But Christianity was not imposed without a struggle: in 1046 Stephen's right-hand man, Bishop Gellért, was murdered by heathens on the hilltop which now bears his name.

As yet, Buda and Pest were insignificant villages. The centre of the kingdom was established, first at Esztergom and later at Székesfehérvár. However, during the 12th century French and German traders were officially encouraged to settle on the banks of the Danube and the future capital began gaining in importance.

Medieval Budapest

Disaster struck in 1241 when the Mongol Golden Horde crossed into Hungary and destroyed Pest. The terrified population fled to Buda but the following winter the Danube froze over and the

Once Buda and Pest were villages on either side of the Danube. Elizabeth Bridge is one of several that connect them, forming the city of Budapest

invaders installed themselves here as well. Things might have been even worse but for the sudden death of the supreme Khan, which led the warlord Batu Khan to return home in order to secure the succession. This unlooked-for breathing space allowed King Béla IV to emerge from hiding and set about improving the defences. Castles were built at various strategic points throughout the country, including Buda. At the same time, German settlers (soon to be joined by Magyar aristocrats) were invited to help repopulate the ravaged town.

The Árpád dynasty died in 1301 and a tussle for the succession ensued. The people of Buda favoured Wenceslas of Bohemia and when the pope expressed a preference for his rival,

BACKGROUND

Charles Robert of Anjou, they 'excommunicated' him in a ceremony held in the Church of Our Lady (now the Matthias Church). While the citizenry lost this particular contest – Charles Robert was eventually imposed on them – they gained when the Royal seat was moved to Buda from Visegrád. During the reigns of Louis (Lajos) I and the King-Emperor Sigismund of Luxembourg (1387–1437) the town flourished as never before. An imposing Gothic Palace rose up alongside the newly rebuilt Castle on the crown of Castle Hill. The ruins now form part of the Budapest History Museum. New religious foundations were erected, including the Dominican church and monastery whose remains have now been incorporated into the modern Hilton Hotel. The Hungarian population,

Pest was destroyed in 1241 by Mongol hordes: it was Béla IV who refounded his nation. Below, modern Pest, seen from Buda

which gravitated towards the north end of Castle Hill near the Magdalen Tower, was effaced by foreign communities of merchants and artisans – French in Fortuna utca, Italians in Országház utca and Germans in the neighbourhood of the Matthias Church. The Jews, too, were here and had their own Prayer House and cemetery.

The Turkish Occupation
Buda reached its apogee in the region of Matthias (Mátyás) Corvinus (1458–90) when the court became a centre of Renaissance learning, boasting one of the largest libraries in Europe. Artists and craftsmen from Italy were invited by the king and his second wife, Beatrice of Aragon (a friend of Lorenzo de Medici) to work on the refurbishment of the royal palace.

BACKGROUND

With Matthias' death, Hungary fell into irreversible decline. His successor, Wladislaw of Bohemia, was weak and vacillating and the nobility took full advantage, arrogantly usurping his authority and pursuing their territorial claims with a suicidal singlemindedness. Oppressed beyond endurance, the impoverished peasants staged a rebellion which was mercilessly suppressed (their leader, György Dózsa, was roasted alive). The divided loyalties inspired by the Reformation reduced the kingdom to anarchy, making it ripe for conquest. In 1526 the Turks, who had been threatening to attack for some time, defeated the Hungarian forces at Mohács. Buda fell in 1541, initiating an occupation that was to last for 150 years.

The Turks have generally had a bad press, but of course their own chroniclers saw things differently. There are some splendid Turkish baths surviving in Budapest but otherwise little of their contribution remains today. They improved the fortifications around the castle but allowed the royal palace and many of the merchant houses to fall into ruin. Most of the churches were turned into mosques.

After sustaining a dozen sieges, Buda was finally recaptured by a joint European force in 1686. Pope Innocent XI, who financed the venture, is given much of the credit and his statue now stands in the centre of Hess András tér.

Hapsburg Budapest

Having shaken off one foreign power, the Hungarians now found themselves dominated by another. The Austrian Hapsburgs ruled from Vienna and discouraged independent activity, though they did allow limited progress in the commercial and industrial spheres. Their major contribution, however, was an architectural one. Buda was rebuilt in the baroque and neo-classical styles then fashionable and inhabited by wealthy Hungarian merchants and princes. But beneath the veneer of wealth and contentment was a growing Hungarian nationalism. From time to time, this erupted into open rebellion. The armed struggle, led by Prince Ferenc Rákóczi II from 1703 to 1711, was eventually defeated, as was the Jacobin conspiracy of 1795, which resulted in the beheading of Ignác Martinovics

Sedilia such as these in the Castle district have been preserved from Buda's medieval days

and his fellow conspirators in what is still known as 'blood meadow' (Vérmező).

In the face of overwhelming odds, violent confrontation was almost bound to end in failure. Acknowledging this painfully acquired lesson, the Reform Movement of the early 19th century sought to pursue similar goals by peaceful means. Its most influential exponent was Count István Széchenyi (1791–1860), a firm believer in material and scientific progress. England was his model: 'England has learned three things that we must learn,' he told his fellow countrymen after returning from one of many visits abroad, 'the constitution, engineering and horse-breeding.'

Constitutional reform had to wait but horse-racing was introduced in 1827. For the first time too, Buda, not Pest, became the main focus of economic and social activity. Hungary's first university had already been transferred here in 1784. In 1802 Ferenc Széchenyi (István's father) conceived the idea of a National Museum, a

BACKGROUND

While much of Buda's charm dates, as above, from the 18th century, it was the 19th century that saw Pest's architectural flowering

project finally realised in 1848. An Academy of Sciences was founded in 1830 and a National Theatre seven years later. Széchenyi himself will always be associated with the Chain Bridge which bears his name, the first permanent link between Buda and Pest, completed under British supervision in 1849.

The era of peaceful reform was destined not to last. In March 1848, following news of rioting in Vienna, crowds began to gather in the centre of Pest. They were addressed from the steps of the National Museum by the self-appointed leaders of the revolution, among them the young poet, Sándor Petőfi, whose famous 'Song' was rapturously received. A newly formed provisional government under Count Lajos Batthyány declared Hungary independent. Backs to the wall, the Austrians made concessions, but early in 1849 the battle was rejoined. At first the

Hungarian forces had the upper hand but Russia's intervention on the side of Austria proved decisive. Retribution was swift. Batthyány and 13 rebel generals were executed. Others suffered torture, imprisonment or exile.
The fortress known as the Citadella, which still dominates the approaches to Gellért Hill, stands as a reminder of the Austrian presence at its most oppressive. In 1867, however, changing circumstances resulted in a change of policy: the *Ausgleich*, or Compromise, granted a measure of autonomy to Hungary within the framework of a Dual Monarchy and ushered in a period of spectacular capitalist development.

Fin de Siècle Budapest

Within 30 years, Budapest (the two towns were amalgamated in 1873) had become one of the leading cities of Europe. The pavement cafés lining new thoroughfares like Andrássy Avenue and the Great Boulevard became the haunt of a self-confident intellectual élite. Tourists from all over Europe patronised the grand hotels jostling for pre-eminence along the Corso (Pest embankment). Migrant workers from the rural hinterland left the slums of the outer city for the giant concerns of Hungary's industrial revolution, Weiss, Ganz and Óbuda Shipbuilding. New bridges spanned the Danube, modern municipal services were introduced, the first underground railway system on the European mainland was constructed and an unprecedented building boom turned the city into a showpiece of architectural eclecticism.
In 1896 the millenary celebrations, marking the thousandth anniversary of the Magyar conquest, took place in Budapest. Thousands of visitors, in holiday mood, came to the City Park to inspect the stands and exhibition tents and to marvel at Alpár's Vajdahunyad Castle. There was an overwhelming atmosphere of self-congratulation in the air, a confidence in Hungary's future, symbolised in that quintessential architectural monument, the Parliament building.

War, Revolution and Independence

World War I shattered these illusions of permanence and prosperity. Shackled to Austria and consequently bound by her alliance with

BACKGROUND

Shortly after its completion, the Art Nouveau Gellért Hotel was taken over by Horthy as his headquarters

Germany, Hungary found herself on the side of the defeated. Amid the ruins of the former Empire, independence was proclaimed and a republic adopted; Mihály Károlyi became the first president in January 1919. But the hold of the new regime was precarious, especially in Budapest where prisoners of war returning from internment in Russia fuelled the discontent of a starving and disease-ridden population. The communists seized power and created a Soviet-style workers' republic under Béla Kun. This in turn collapsed after 133 days when the nationalist, Admiral Miklós Horthy led an army of 25,000 into Budapest and established his headquarters in the Gellért Hotel.

Horthy's authoritarian rule and his determination to regain the territories lost in the post-war settlement, made him a natural ally of the Nazis and in 1941 Hungary entered World War II on

Chapel of Ják, Vajdahunyad Castle, in City Park. The castle was built for the millenary exhibition of 1896

the side of Germany. However, growing doubts about Horthy's reliability led to the occupation of Budapest in March 1944. The inevitable persecution of Jews, Communists and other anti-Fascists was followed in the autumn by a reign of terror masterminded by the Hungarian Arrow Cross. Thousands of Jews were deported but thanks to the intervention of the young Swedish attaché, Raoul Wallenberg, some at least avoided the death camps. Wallenberg himself disappeared in the chaos of the final months of the war. By the time the Soviets took control in February 1945, the city was in ruins.

People's Republic
In the post-war years, Communist rule was consolidated under Stalin's henchman, Mátyás Rákosi and the country was collectivised and industrialised on the Soviet model. A

A decorative reminder of Buda's more grandiose days

reconstructed Budapest rose from the ashes but life in the capital remained grim. Show trials, political repression and economic hardship were the main ingredients in the explosive mix which detonated the Hungarian Uprising of October 1956. All the principal events took place in Budapest – the march of 50,000 protesters from Bem József tér to Parliament, the siege of the radio building, the beheading of Stalin's statue near the City Park and the fighting itself. The tanks rolled in on 4 November and ruthlessly crushed resistance. Thousands were executed and some 200,000 Hungarians fled into exile. But the impact of the uprising was huge, and change was inevitable. The new leader, János Kádár, gradually brought about a transition from political totalitarianism to a consensus between leadership and people. His 32-year rule finally ended when he was ousted from power in 1988.

A New Start

Today Budapest is a happier place as its people throw off the shackles of Soviet occupation, removing the red stars from the Parliament building and from the park on Gellért Hill, renaming the streets and rehabilitating formerly disgraced politicians like Imre Nagy. As Hungary's new government bids to become a member of the European Community, Budapest faces west, hopefully towards a brighter future.

WHAT TO SEE

The places of interest described here are listed alphabetically in three sections – Buda, Pest, and Around Budapest.

Included are some of the 70 or more museums and 70 galleries in Budapest, catering for the specialist and general visitor alike. Opening times are the latest available, but it is a good idea to check at the information desk of your hotel before setting out. Subjects range from philately to pharmacy, from fine arts to transport. As in most countries of Eastern Europe, the displays are often unimaginatively presented, but the most serious drawback is the absence of catalogues and information in English (or in most other European languages). Hopefully, the recent social and political changes in Hungary will lead to improvements here also.

For special exhibitions, see the monthly brochures *Programme in Hungary* or *Budapest Panorama* available at Tourist Information Centres.

Buda

The delights of historical Buda make it the first port of call of every tourist. You will want to begin with a view from Pest across the Danube and there are two ideal vantage points. Probably the better (and slightly less spoiled by the constant roar of traffic) is from Széchenyi rakpart in front of the Országház (Parliament building). From here you will easily be able to pick out the spire of the Mátyás-templom (Matthias Church) on top of Várhegy (Castle Hill) and the outline of the Víziváros (Watertown) district below. From nearby Kóssuth Lajos tér you can take Metro line 2 across the river to Batthyány tér, then

Buda, with Matthias Church and Fishermen's Bastion, seen from Pest

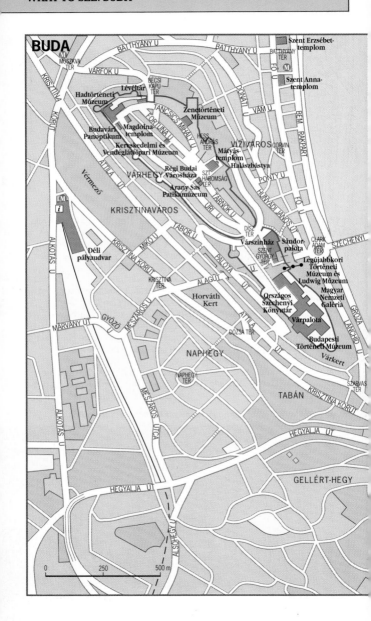

walk along Fő utca and climb one of the narrow streets up to Halászbástya (Fishermen's Bastion).

Alternatively, you can cross by the Széchenyi lánchíd (Chain Bridge), the other excellent viewing point, and pick up the funicular railway (Budavári Sikló) from Clark Ádám tér. (Buy your ticket at the turnstile). On a hot day this saves a tiring climb, but you may have to queue. Good for views and photographs of Pest as you go up.

A third approach is to take the No. 16 bus from Erzsébet tér, which winds its way up Castle Hill to Dísz tér (also handy for the Royal Palace and museums).

◆
ARANY SAS PATIKAMÚZEUM (GOLDEN EAGLE PHARMACY MUSEUM)

Tárnok utca 18
All the tools of the pharmaceutical trade, dating back to the Middle Ages, are exhibited here. The house itself is 15th-century and there has been a pharmacy on the premises for more than 200 years.
Open: Tuesday to Sunday 10.30–18.00 hrs
Closed: Monday

◆◆
BUDAPESTI TÖRTÉNETI MÚZEUM (BUDAPEST HISTORY MUSEUM)

Royal Palace, Castle Hill
Occupying the southern end of the former Royal Palace, Wing E, the museum is divided into two sections. The remains of the medieval palace, together with

sculptures, ceramics, pots and pans, and weapons can be seen on the lower floor, a maze of labyrinthine passageways, cellars and vaulted halls. Above is an exhibition devoted to the 2,000-year history of Budapest, containing the usual array of photographs, prints and posters and, more unusually, survivals from the Turkish occupation. Unfortunately, there is no English language commentary. **Legújabbkori Történeti Múzeum (Museum of Contemporary History)** situated in the opposite, northern wing of the palace (Wing A); a branch of the Hungarian National Museum, it features temporary exhibitions concerning Hungary's recent past. Also in Wing A (on the first floor), **Ludwig Múzeum (Ludwig Museum)**, is dedicated to international contemporary art.
Open: Budapest History Museum, Wednesday to Monday 10.00–18.00 hrs
Closed: Tuesday.
Open: Museum of Contemporary History and Ludwig Museum, Tuesday to Sunday 10.00–17.30 hrs (Ludwig 17.00 hrs)
Closed: Monday.

Gellért monument, Gellért Hill

◆◆◆
GELLÉRT-HEGY (GELLÉRT HILL) ✓

The best vantage point from which to see Budapest, Gellért Hill looms over the Castle District, rising to a height of 430 feet (130m) between the Erzsébet (Elizabeth) and Szabadság (Freedom) Bridges. Vines used to grow on these rugged slopes but a phylloxera epidemic mid-way through the last century killed off the entire crop. There are numerous points of access; the most direct approach is to take any one of the footpaths which wind their way around the hill in the vicinity of Elizabeth Bridge. Alternatively, the No. 27 bus will take you to the top from Móricz Zsigmond körtér. If you have a car, you can take one of the side roads around Szirtes út, which leads directly to the Citadella (taxis are available at both these points). The hill is named after Bishop Gellért (Gerard), who was summoned from Italy by King Stephen to help convert the Magyars to Christianity. A massive statue of the saint, framed by a semi-circular colonnade, overlooks the Elizabeth Bridge from the spot where, it is said, a group of obdurate heathens cast him off in a barrel during a rebellion several years after the king's death. Defiant to the last, the grim-faced bronze figure raises a cross high above the city. An artificial waterfall runs below. At the bottom of the hill, on the Szent Gellért rakpart, are the **Rudas Baths(Rudas Fürdő)**, part of which date from the time of the Turkish occupation. Built by Pasha Mustapha in 1566, an octagonal pool has a magnificent domed roof.

The **Citadella**, on the crown of the hill, is a fortress of white stone constructed by the Austrians to quell the population in the aftermath of the 1848–9 War of Independence. Gaps were later made in the walls to symbolise the restoration of good relations following the Compromise of 1867.Today it is home to a restaurant and dormitary-style hotel.

Szabadság szobor (Freedom Monument), beside the Citadella, overlooking the river, was built to commemorate the Soviet-led liberation of Budapest from the Nazis in 1945. The designer was a Hungarian, Zsigmond Kisfaludi-Strobl, but the inscription on the base is in Russian and reads: 'To the liberating Soviet heroes from a grateful Hungarian people'. The statue of the Socialist-realist heroine, holding a palm in both hands, is one of the city's landmarks, a role which will probably save it from the fate of the metal red star which was removed recently from the nearby park. Away from the monument in the direction of the Freedom Bridge, is Szent Gellért tér, where the famous **Hotel Gellért** and the **Gellért Fürdő** are situated. The hotel, in Art Nouveau style, was once the headquarters of the Hungarian dictator, Admiral Horthy. On the slopes of Gellért Hill you can see the houses and apartments of some of the well-heeled inhabitants of present-day Budapest.

◆
HADTÖRTÉNETI MÚZEUM (MUSEUM OF MILITARY HISTORY)

Tóth Árpád sétány 40
A former barracks, the museum contains exhibits relating to the whole history of armed strife in Hungary.
Open: Tuesday to Saturday 09.00–17.00 hrs (10.00–16.00 in winter), Sunday 10.00–18.00 hrs
Closed: Monday

◆◆◆
HALÁSZBÁSTYA (FISHERMEN'S BASTION) ✓

Castle Hill
On the eastern edge of Castle Hill, near the Mátyás-templom (Matthias Church), this entertaining architectural fantasy was built at the end of the 19th century to coincide with the city's 1,000th anniversary celebrations. The designer was Frigyes Schulek, who obviously enjoyed letting his imagination run riot after toiling away at church restoration. It gets its name from the fishermen of the Víziváros (Watertown) district who traditionally defended this section of the fortifications. The seven tent-shaped turrets represent the seven Hungarian tribes who made their home here. Walk along the parapets to get a superb view of the city and river (smog permitting). No marks for spotting the Parliament building and the unmistakable dome of St Stephen's Church. Lined up along the embankment (the Corso) you should also be able to make out three of Pest's premier hotels: the Atrium Hyatt, the Forum and the Duna. The Széchenyi lánchíd (Chain Bridge) spans the river near by. On your left, in the distance, is the tree-shrouded Margit-sziget (Margaret Island). The arches and recesses of the Bastion provide welcome shade from the hot summer sun and an opportunity to rest the legs. It is also a good place to write those postcards home. The stalls selling lace and other crafted articles have tourists in mind and the prices may therefore be on the steep side. On the other hand, buy a few presents here now and it may save you a lot of foot-slogging later.

◆
MAGYAR KERESKEDELMI ÉS VENDÉGLÁTÓIPARI MÚZEUM (MUSEUM OF HUNGARIAN COMMERCE AND CATERING)

Fortuna utca 4
Occupying the premises of an 18th-century inn, this charming small museum deals with Hungarian confectionery as well as 19th/20th century commerce. It is far more interesting than it sounds!
Open: Tuesday to Sunday 10.00–18.00 hrs
Closed: Monday

◆◆
MAGYAR NEMZETI GALÉRIA (HUNGARIAN NATIONAL GALLERY)

Royal Palace, Castle Hill
Four floors of the former Royal Palace are devoted to all aspects of Hungarian art and sculpture from medieval times to the present day. The collection includes altarpieces, wood panels and paintings dating from

Fishermen's Bastion

the 15th and 16th centuries; work by the important 19th-century artist Mihály Munkácsy (once renowned throughout Europe and honoured with a hero's funeral in Budapest), Pál Szinyei Merse, and László Paál; and some interesting 20th-century paintings showing the influence of the Western Cubist and Expressionist schools on Béla Czóbel, Lajos Tihanyi and Lajos Kassák, among others.
Open: Tuesday to Sunday 10.00–18.00 hrs
Closed: Monday

◆◆◆
MÁTYÁS-TEMPLOM
(MATTHIAS CHURCH) ✓

Szentháromság tér (Trinity Square)

Founded by King Béla IV in about 1250, the church – actually dedicated to the Virgin Mary – takes its name from Mátyás (Matthias) Corvinus, who added the finishing touches in the second half of the 15th century. The Turks turned it into a mosque, removing the furnishings and white-washing the walls. Two chandeliers from the high altar can still be seen in Saint Sohpia's in Istanbul. The Jesuits celebrated the reconsecration of the church by fitting it out in sumptuous baroque style. They also built a college next door, where the Hilton Hotel now stands. By the 19th century, urgent repairs were needed to the church's exterior. One of Hungary's most distinguished architects, Frigyes Schulek, undertook the restoration, which was completed in 1896. Very little of the original building now remains. The church has been the setting for many famous historical events. It was here in 1302 that the citizens of Buda 'excommunicated' Pope Boniface VIII for daring to support Charles Robert of Anjou's claim to the throne over that of their own candidate, Wenceslas of Bohemia. Matthias Corvinus married Beatrice of Aragon here in the 15th century, and it was here also that the last Hapsburg rulers, Franz Josef I and Charles IV were crowned, in 1867 and 1916 respectively.

Enter the church through the Mary Portal where you can still see a 14th-century relief depicting the death of the Virgin. The main body of the church is 19th-century but the dazzling interior decoration with its painted floral motifs is based on the original medieval designs. The church has strong musical associations. Liszt's *Coronation Mass* and Kodály's *Te Deum* were both first performed here and the tradition continues with regular concerts and recitals (Friday evenings in the summer, tickets available at the door). On Sundays there is a sung high mass at 10.00, sometimes with orchestral accompaniment. In the Loreto Chapel, to the left of the Mary Portal as you go in, there is a Gothic triptych and a baroque black madonna dating from about 1700. Note the original coat of arms of Matthias Corvinus (The Raven) on the wall by the main altar. The chapel nearest the main door on the opposite side of the church is dedicated to St Imre, son of the first Christian king of Hungary, St Stephen. Next to it is the Holy Trinity chapel, where you will find the tomb of the 12th-century king, Béla III, and his wife, Anne of Chatillon, although their remains were moved here only in 1848. The two oratories, the chapel of St Stephen and the crypt (access to the side of the main pulpit) all contain exhibits from the Ecclesiastical Art Collection. To the side of the church is a large equestrian statue of St Stephen (note the cross and halo).

Matthias Church

◆◆◆
VÁRHEGY (CASTLE HILL)

*Closed to cars (except to residents
and Hilton Hotel guests).*

You can easily spend a day in the Várnegyed, or Castle district. It is probably best to visit the more picturesque streets (see below) in the morning, before the crowds arrive, and leave the Royal Palace and museums for the afternoon.

Buda and Pest were distinct communities until they were joined, by administrative fiat, in 1873 and they are still as different in appearance as chalk and cheese. Buda stretches rather lazily along the slopes of Castle Hill, a mile-long plateau of craggy limestone overlooking the Danube from a height of 200 feet (60m). Its history has been troubled and turbulent. The first settlement here was destroyed by the Mongols in 1241, inducing Béla IV, somewhat belatedly, to improve the defences. He built a castle and the citizens made new homes for themselves around the royal quarters. A thriving community developed and, by the beginning of the 16th century, Buda was known throughout Europe as a centre of Renaissance learning. Dark times were about to return, however. The Turks were already knocking at the gates and in 1541 they seized the castle, beginning an occupation which was to last almost 150 years. Buda then fell into decline. The Royal Palace was abandoned and most of the inhabitants fled, the churches were despoiled and turned into mosques. On the positive side, the invaders improved the fortifications and built the bath houses which are still a tourist attraction today. The Turks were finally expelled in 1686 but recovery was slow and Buda never really regained its old importance. Its charm today stems from a decision of the new Austrian rulers to rebuild from scratch in the baroque style, and the uniform elegance which resulted makes its streets a delight to stroll in. It is hard to believe that all this is the product of painstaking restoration work following the town's almost total destruction at the end of World War II.

Út, utca and tér (streets and squares) of the Castle District
Dísz tér, once known as Pasha Square (a reminder of the Turkish occupation), was formerly a parade ground. The statue of the soldier commemorates the heroes of the War of Independence of 1848–9. **Tárnok utca** is one of the most attractive streets in Buda. As with most of the streets here, the houses are largely of 18th-century design, built on medieval foundations and still retaining fragments of the earlier features. The word *tárnok* means treasurer and the street was once the hub of Buda's commercial life. The building with the rusty patterning at No. 14 dates from the 14th and 15th centuries (the protruding first floor was the medieval hall). Adjoining it at No.16 is the wine bar and restaurant called the Arany Hordó (Golden Barrel). No. 18 is the **Arany Sas Patikamúzeum (Golden Eagle Pharmacy Museum)** (see entry on page 23). The original building dates from the 15th century. **Szent Háromság tér**

Fortunautca, one of Castle Hill's picturesque streets

WHAT TO SEE: BUDA

(Trinity Square) is named after the monument to the Holy Trinity in the centre. It was erected by the grateful survivors of a plague in the 18th century. The building at No. 7 is the famous **Ruszwurm pastry shop**, which has been producing mouth-watering aromas since it opened in 1827. The two-storey baroque building on the corner of Szent Háromság utca is the old Buda Town Hall. You will also be able to see Halászbástya (Fishermen's Bastion) and part of the Hilton Hotel. But the dominant feature of the square is undoubtedly the **Mátyás-templom (Matthias**

Castle Hill's picturesque streets are good for browsing

Church) (see separate entry). **Hess András tér** passes in front of the Hilton Hotel. The hotel was built in 1976 on the site of a Dominican church and monastery. In keeping with modern architectural fashion, the ruins have been incorporated into the overall design. The main front of the hotel also bears traces of the 18th-century Jesuit college which used to stand here. Not everyone appreciates this peculiar mix of old and new, but the Hilton, which has recently been spruced up, is the focus of Buda nightlife and so cannot be ignored. Charming Hess András tér gets its name from Hungary's first printer, who had a shop here in the 15th century. The statue in

the middle is of Pope Innocent XI who inspired the Christians to defeat and finally expel the Turks in the 1680s. The 18th-century building to the rear of the statue is a former inn called the Red Hedgehog (you can see its delightful emblem over the main door). There were originally three medieval houses on the site and you can still see traces of them in the main door and window frames. There is now an antiques shop here. **Táncsics Mihály utca**, is named after one of the heroes of the 1848 uprising. The elegant building at No. 7 was once an 18th-century palace and is now the **Zenetörténeti Múzeum (Music History Museum)** (see

entry below). Even if you don't want to visit the museum, at least have a look at the splendid baroque courtyard. Beethoven stayed here when he visited Buda to give a series of concerts in 1800. Another musical genius, the Hungarian composer Béla Bartók, later set up a workshop here and the museum displays some of his autographed scores. No. 9 has at various times served as royal mint, barracks and prison. During the War of Independence with the Austrians, many leading revolutionaries, including Táncsics and his more famous comrade-in-arms, Lajos Kossuth, were incarcerated in the dungeons here. The yellow building at No. 16 has an attractive 18th-century mural between the windows on the first floor. No. 26 reminds us that this was once the Jewish quarter of the town. There are ancient tombstones on display in this house which once served as a synagogue and is now a museum. At the end of the street is the Bécsi kapu or Vienna Gate, a reconstruction built in 1936 to mark the 250th anniversary of the expulsion of the Turks from Buda. The German novelist, Thomas Mann, lived in the square, at No. 7, from 1935 to 1936.

Fortuna utca is named after an 18th-century inn which used to be situated at No. 4. The building is now occupied by the **Magyar Kereskedelmi és Vendéglátóipari Múzeum (Museum of Hungarian Commerce and Catering)** (see seperate entry).

Országház utca, or Parliament

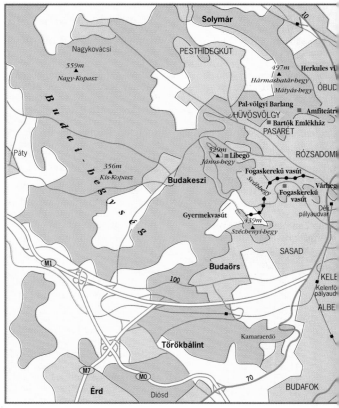

Street, is a reminder of the days when Buda was much more than an oversized, if picturesque, museum. During the 1790s both Houses of the Hungarian Diet, or Parliament, met at No. 28, so conditions must have been fairly cramped. No. 2, now a restaurant, occupies the site of a 15th-century mansion. The cloister-like courtyard contains many clues to its medieval past, such as the sedilia (stone seats) in the doorway and the surviving stone arches. The houses at Nos. 18, 20 and 22 are also medieval in origin, although all have been heavily reconstructed.
Kapisztrán tér is at the far end of the street, dominated by the 13th-century Magdalene tower, sadly all that now remains of the church of that name. The yellow building at No. 40 is the **Hadtörténeti Múzeum (Museum of Military History)** (see entry).

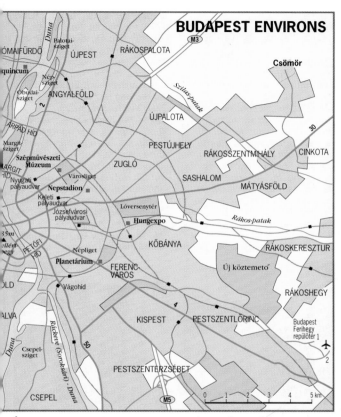

BUDAPEST ENVIRONS

Úri utca's courtyards (particularly Nos. 31, 32, 34, 36, 38 and 40) contain more medieval remnants, No. 31 being the best preserved of all. A visit to the **Budavári Panoptikum (Buda Castle Labyrinth Waxworks)**, situated at No. 9, is the only way nowadays to see what remains of the underground passageways and caves that used to criss-cross beneath the town. Turks and Christians alike made good use of them as a means of deploying troops and surprising enemies. Later, they were converted into cellars which made ideal air-raid shelters during World War II. Now a waxworks depicts scenes from Magyar history. *Open:* Wednesday to Monday 10.00-18.00 hrs.

Tóth Árpád sétány, the western ramparts of the Castle District, offer a good view of the Buda hills.

◆◆◆
VÁRPALOTA
(THE ROYAL PALACE) ✓

Castle Hill

The Royal Palace, razed to the ground and rebuilt countless times, suffered some degree of destruction and reconstruction with every twist and turn of Buda's equally turbulent history. It was originally built in the second half of the 13th century by Béla IV after the invasion of the Mongols. The Angevin kings later enlarged it; the recently discovered foundations of the István tower, plus the reconstructed crypt of the Royal chapel, are relics of those times. Under the Holy Roman Emperor Sigismund of Luxembourg (king of Hungary from the late 14th century to the mid-15th century) the palace was enlarged again, this time in the Gothic style. Today sections from this time, such as the vast Knights Hall, have been reconstructed. When King Matthias (Mátyás) (1458–90) came to the throne, then began what is generally regarded as the golden age of the Palace (and of Buda generally). Most of the castle was rebuilt in the Italian Renaissance style and new buildings were added; many politicians, artists and scholars visited the Palace

The Museum of Music History where Béla Bartók had his workshop

as it became known as a centre of European culture (and a place where the hospitality was lavish). When the Turks invaded they did little damage to the great Renaissance edifice but it was finally and tragically destroyed during the great siege of 1686. The Austrian Hapsburgs became Hungary's new rulers in the early 18th century and they levelled the ruins of the former magnificent edifice and began work on a smaller palace of their own. In 1800 Joseph Haydn conducted his oratorio *The Creation* in the ceremonial hall of the new palace. Throughout the 19th century the palace was expanded and renovated (one of the wings and the middle of the palace was destroyed by fire in 1849). The neo-baroque form that the building took on was the work of the architect Miklós Ybl (he added the building which today houses the Széchényi National Library). Alajos Hauszmann took over as architect when Ybl died and completed the construction of the symmetrical palace building in 1905.

The troubles were not over though; in World War II the palace was completely burnt out. Work began on reconstruction in the 1950s – it was only completed during the 1980s. Remains of the original, medieval palace were found and can be seen by visitors today. The renovated Palace was built with modern interiors to house cultural and state institutions; several major museums can be seen within its confines, including the **Magyar Nemzeti Galéria (Hungarian National Gallery)**, the **Budapesti Történeti Múzeum (Budapest History Museum/Castle Museum)**, the **Legújabbkori Történeti Múzeum (Museum of Contemporary History)** and the **Ludwig Múzeum (Ludwig Museum)** (see separate entries on pages 23–24).

Leaving via the northern end of the Palace complex, note the impressive yellow building marked **Várszínház** between Szent György tér and adjoining Dísz tér. This is the **Castle Theatre**. Originally a church, it was redesigned in the 1780s. Shortly afterwards, the first Hungarian theatre company began performing here. The relief just inside the entrance commemorates a concert given by Beethoven in 1800.

◆
ZENETÖRTÉNETI MÚZEUM (MUSEUM OF MUSIC HISTORY)
Táncsics Mihály utca 7
As the entrance to this imposing building suggests, it once belonged to a Hungarian nobleman. Beethoven lived here for a while in 1800, and the 20th-century Hungarian composer, Béla Bartók, set up a workshop on the premises. On display are a motley collection of old instruments manufactured in Hungary (including some splendid examples of folk instruments) as well as a special exhibition on the life and work of Bartók. All this would be fascinating if only there was a translation.
Open: Monday 16.00–21.00 hrs; Wednesday to Sunday 10.00–18.00 hrs
Closed: Tuesday

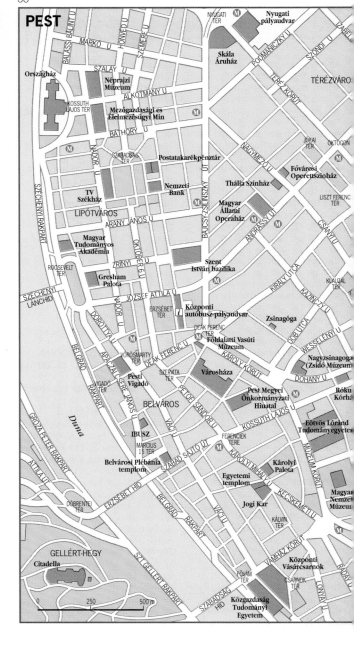

PEST

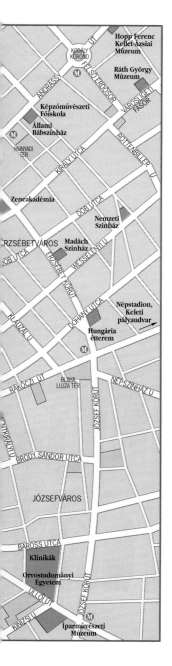

Pest

While there have been settlers
on the right bank of the Danube
since ancient times, the present
appearance of Pest
(pronounced *pesht* by
Hungarians) owes most to the
period from 1840 onwards when
the city became the focus of a
cultural renewal inspired by
anti-Austrian resistance.
Following the Compromise of
1867, Pest was transformed,
along with Buda, into an imperial
capital equal in status with
Vienna. But virtually all the
subsequent construction boom
was concentrated on the right
bank and the Art Nouveau and
Eclectic styles then fashionable
have left their indelible mark on
the city. The great stone
embankment known as the
Corso, already a favourite with
promenaders, was now lined
with a series of grandiose
hotels, each more opulent than
the last. Today only the names
have changed. Hungary's
enhanced political status was
encapsulated in the huge
Parliament building (then
claimed to be the largest in the
world) which rose up near by.
Government, banking and
insurance offices and the largest
stock exchange in Europe
added to Pest's growing sense
of self-importance. New bridges
were built across the Danube
and the first underground
railway on the European
mainland was built beneath
Andrássy út. This resplendent
thoroughfare became the
linchpin of a network of
boulevards and ringroads which
still exists, although the names
have undergone various

changes. Pest is inextricably linked to the more dramatic moments in Hungary's modern history. The poet Petőfi proclaimed the country's independence from the steps of the National Museum in 1848. Béla Kun established a short-lived Soviet republic here in 1919. A quarter of a century later, German and Soviet troops were fighting over every square yard of the city (you can still see the bullet holes in the Jewish district). And the former radio building and secret police headquarters are reminders of the ill-starred Hungarian revolution of 1956. Today, Pest is a city to stroll and browse in – don't make the mistake of trying to cover too much ground at

The sumptuous State Opera House

once. If you get tired of sightseeing, there's always the restful Városliget (City Park) or any of the numerous cafés and bars which line the main avenues. And Pest's modern shopping streets, with their eye-catching displays, make it a home-from-home for Westerners.

◆◆◆
ÁLLAMI OPERAHÁZ (STATE OPERA HOUSE) ✓

Andrássy út 22
One of the most important buildings in the history of Hungarian architecture, the State Opera House in Budapest also ranks among the most beautiful in Europe; its interior possibly the richest in the city. The Emperor Franz Josef commissioned Miklós Ybl to design an opera house for Budapest to compete with the finest in Europe; he certainly achieved this and in doing so produced what is considered by many to be his *opus magnum*. Construction began in 1875; marbled, gilded and decorated with frescos by some of the finest painters of the time, this elegant neo-Renaissance building opened nine years later in 1884. Standards were high from the first: Gustav Mahler was Music Director for a time and, after World War II, so was Otto Klemperer. Its last great director was János Ferencsik who died in 1984.
The balconied façade of the building is adorned with statues of the great composers: Monteverdi, Scarlatti, Gluck, Mozart, Beethoven, Rossini, Donizetti, Glinka, Wagner, Verdi, Gounod, Bizet, Mussorgsky, Tchaikovsky, Moniusko and Smetana. First-floor niches hold Terpsichore, Erato, Thalia and Melpomene, to represent dance, love-poetry, comedy and tragedy.
Inside the vast auditorium, seating an audience of around 1,300 and facing a stage 47 yards (43m) deep, a three-ton, bronze chandelier hangs from a ceiling decorated with a fine fresco by Károly Lotz; it shows Greek Gods with Apollo, the God of Music in the centre.
Other paintings in the public rooms include those by Mór Than and Bertalan Székely. While Budapest's opera house was under construction, a particularly tragic fire destroyed the Ringtheatre in Vienna, killing over 400 people. As a result, all-metal, hydraulic stage machinery, an iron curtain and sprinkler system were installed in Budapest's new opera house. It was the most modern theatre in the world. Closed in 1981 for extensive renovations, the opera house was re-opened in all its former magnificence on 27 September 1984: exactly one hundred years after the first performance was given here.
The box office is open weekdays 11.00–13.45 and 14.30–18.30 hrs; Saturday 11.00–18.30 hrs; Sunday 10.00–14.00 hrs for morning performances, 16.00–19.00 hrs for evening performances; seats may be available on the day of a performance but you may get a seat without a view of the stage! Visits to the Opera House outside performance hours can only be made daily by guided tours at 15.00 and 16.00 hrs.

◆◆◆
ANDRÁSSY ÚT/OKTOGON/KODÁLY KÖRÖND

In the days of Franz Josef this elegant avenue, then named after the statesman, Andrássy, was the most fashionable promenading route in Budapest. At one time known as Stalin Avenue, it was until recently called the Avenue of the People's Republic. It runs all the way from Deák tér to Városliget (City Park). The first section was built in the 1870s for rich citizens and prosperous businessmen, whose inflated tastes are reflected in the variety of rather ponderous architectural styles.

Állami Operaház (State Opera House) No. 22, was designed by the famous 19th- century Hungarian architect, Miklós Ybl in neo-Renaissance style. It has recently undergone major restoration to celebrate its 100th anniversary. Opposite is the State Ballet School.

Oktogon is the first major intersection. Originally called Octagon Square in the days when a blue flag flying from the mast of the Skating Club meant that the lake in the City Park was sufficiently frozen over for skating, it was renamed after Mussolini from 1938 to 1945 and until recently it was named November 7 tér to commemorate the Russian Revolution. At No. 60, is the former headquarters of the secret police where victims of the Stalinist terror, and later of the Hungarian uprising, were taken to be interrogated and tortured.

The **Liszt Ferenc Zeneművészeti Főiskola/Zeneakadémia (Academy of Music)** is across the road at List Ferenc tér 8. The Hungarian composer Ferenc (Franz) Liszt, of *Hungarian Rhapsody* fame, founded the Academy in 1875 and lived here as its first director from 1881 until his death five years later. The building is in Art Nouveau style, with a statue of Liszt above the main entrance. **The Állami Bábszínház (State Puppet Theatre)** and the **Képzőművészeti Főiskola (Academy of Fine Arts)** occupy the buildings at Nos. 69–71 Andrássy út. **Kodály körönd**, an elegant crescent composed of four neo-Renaissance palaces in a leafy setting, is named after Zoltán Kodály (1882–1967), composer, music researcher and teacher who lived at No. 89 and whose memorial museum is at No. 1. In the days before World War I, the villas of the final, tree-lined section of the Avenue were the exclusive preserve of the richest Hungarians, including members of the Magyar aristocracy. (The British Consulate was also here.) For the remainder of Andrássy út see **Hősök tere (Heroes' Square)** and **Városliget (City Park)**.

◆
ÁRPÁD HÍD (ÁRPÁD BRIDGE)

The longest of the six bridges crossing the Danube in the vicinity of downtown Budapest, it links the mainland with Margit-sziget (Margaret Island).

◆◆
BELVÁROSI PLÉBÁNIA TEMPLOM (INNER CITY PARISH CHURCH)

Március 15 tér
March 15 Square (the Revolution

A corner of Kodály körönd

of 1848 began on that day) is situated at the Pest end of Elizabeth Bridge. This was the centre of the 4th-century Roman settlement of Contra-Aquincum. There is a small display of some of the remains. Hard against the flyover you will find one of the most attractive buildings in the city, the so-called Inner City Parish Church. Dating from the 12th century, it is also the oldest. However, it was rebuilt in the 14th century and again, after a fire, in the 18th century. This explains the baroque façade and interior. At one time, the Turks used it as a mosque and you can still see a Muslim prayer niche or *mihrab* to the right of the high altar.

◆◆
DOHÁNY UTCA (JEWISH DISTRICT)

At the intersection of Dohány utca and Károly körút (Metro line 2 Astoria), at the heart of the old Jewish quarter, is the recently restored Synagogue (the largest in Europe). The style of this 19th-century building is Moorish-Byzantine (note the minaret-style towers). The **Zsidó Múzeum**

(Jewish Museum) (see below) is here. The streets running between Dohány utca and Dob utca (Síp, Kazinczy, Nagy Diófa, Rumbach, Klauzál utca) are a living memorial to the once-thriving community which was persecuted during World War II. Bullet marks scar the walls of the grimy apartment blocks which also bear Hebrew plaques and tablets commemorating the thousands of families who perished here. (Many of the survivors owe their lives to the Swedish diplomat, Raoul Wallenberg, who worked fearlessly on their behalf before disappearing into a Soviet labour camp at the end of the war.) The entrance ways and courtyards are worth exploring for their period flavour but one cannot help walking away in a sombre frame of mind. Budapest's seventh district (once the most crowded in the entire city) is very much a working class area and Dob utca contains a number of humble but welcoming *étterems* (restaurants) and bars which provide an interesting window on to everyday urban life.

◆
ERZSÉBET HÍD (ELIZABETH BRIDGE)
This bridge is named after the much-loved Empress Elizabeth, the wife of Franz Josef, who was murdered by an anarchist in 1898. The first bridge, built at the turn of the century, was destroyed during World War II. Its replacement, a modern suspension bridge completed in 1964, owes nothing to the original design.

◆◆
FÖLDALATTI VASÚTI MÚZEUM(UNDERGROUND RAILWAY MUSEUM)
Deák tér
Hidden away in the metro station underpass, this tiny museum occupies one of the

Elizabeth Bridge, and Buda beyond

original railway tunnels. A fascinating array of plans, drawings, models and carriages traces the development of the first underground system on the European mainland. The first line, completed in 1896, ran the entire length of Andrássy út, a distance of two miles (3.5km).
Open: Tuesday to Sunday 10.00–18.00 hrs
Closed: Monday

◆◆
GYÓGYFÜRDŐ (THERMAL BATHS)

For 2,000 years the mineral waters of the hills around Budapest have been appreciated for their therapeutic effects and today the hot springs are enjoyed as much as ever (see **How to be a Local**). Architecturally, the baths make some of Budapest's greatest monuments, and even if you do not 'take the waters', it is worth taking a look at some of the buildings. Bathhouses such as

the **Király** (84 Fő út), **Lukács** (25–9 Frankel Leó út), and **Rudas** (9 Döbrentei tér) survive from the Turkish period of the 16th and 17th centuries. The popular **Gellért** baths (Gellért tér) are housed in a splendid Art Nouveau building dating from the early 20th century, the same period as the elegant **Széchenyi** baths in Állatkerti körút.

◆
HOPP FERENC KELET-ÁZSIAI MÚZEUM (HOPP FERENC EASTERN ASIAN MUSEUM)

Andrássy út 103
The museum houses the oriental treasures amassed by the Hungarian traveller, Ferenc Hopp (1833–1919) who once lived here. The Chinese and Japanese exhibits are housed in the **Ráth György Múzeum** at 12 Városligeti fasor, extension a short walk away.
Open: Tuesday to Sunday

10.00–18.00 hrs
Closed: Monday
Metro: Kodály körönd (line 1)

◆◆◆
HŐSÖK TERE
(HEROES' SQUARE) ✓

A millenary extravaganza, the central feature of Heroes' Square is a 118ft (36m) high column, surmounted by a statue of the Archangel Gabriel; it was supposedly as a result of his intervention that Pope Sylvester II sent a crown to King Stephen. Circling the pedestal are seven figures on horseback, representing the chieftains of the seven Magyar tribes who overran Hungary in 896. The statues which stand in between the columns of the surrounding colonnade honour major figures in the nation's history, including King Stephen and Kossuth. Below each statue is a relief illustrating some significant scene from the life of the person above. After World War II the statues of the Hapsburg rulers were replaced by the Hungarian champions of freedom. The four groups of symbolic figures on the top of the colonnade represent War and Peace, Work and Wealth and

The monument in Heroes' Square

Knowledge and Glory. In front of the monument stands a vast stone tablet: the Hungarian War Memorial, which bears the inscription 'In memory of the heroes who sacrificed their lives for our nation's freedom and for national independence'. The square used to be park-like with trees and bushes; now it boasts ornamental paving, originally laid out in 1938 for the 34th International Eucharistic Congress. The open area adjoining Heroes' Square is known as Procession Square: mass meetings, processions and parades are held here on national and public holidays. It was the site of a monolithic statue of Stalin but during the 1956 revolution this was dragged away, smashed and set alight – a frenzied reassertion of Hungarian nationalism which was captured on contemporary newsreel. Today, soldiers from the former Soviet Union are among those who pay their respects at the Tomb of the Unknown Warrior. The two neo-classical buildings overlooking the square are the **Szépművészti Múzeum (Museum of Fine Arts)** (see entry) and the **Műcsarnok Exhibition Hall.**

◆◆
IPARMŰVÉSZETI MÚZEUM
(MUSEUM OF APPLIED ARTS)
Üllői út 33–7
The original building was one of hundreds hastily erected to mark the millenial celebrations of 1896. It was destroyed during World War II and rebuilt in the 1950s. Designed by Ödön Lechner and Gyula Pártos, the coloured ceramic and brick building blends an Art Nouveau style with Hungarian folk motifs. The interior is also fine, with a glass-roofed hall supported by white crenellated arches. There are separate collections of furniture, metalwork, textiles, woodwork, ceramics and glass, leatherwork, books and paper and other handicrafts.
Open: Tuesday to Sunday 10.00–18.00 hrs
Closed: Monday
Metro: Ferenc körút (line 3)

◆
KŐZLEKEDÉSI MÚZEUM
(TRANSPORT MUSEUM)
Városliget körut 11, Városliget
You can combine a visit here with a stroll across the Városliget (City Park). Ideal for younger visitors, the exhibits include models of ships, cars, trains, motorbikes, aeroplanes and engines. An old railway dining car now serves as a restaurant.
Open: Tuesday to Friday 10.00–16.00, Saturday and Sunday 10.00–18.00 hrs
Closed: Monday
Trolleybus: 72 from Bajcsy-Zsilinszky

◆◆
MAGYAR NEMZETI MÚZEUM
(HUNGARIAN NATIONAL MUSEUM)
Múzeum körút 14–16
From the steps of the museum the 19th-century poet, Sándor Petőfi, proclaimed his 'National Song', an event which heralded the 1848 revolution. Arranged to trace the history of Hungary and its peoples, the exhibits of every shape, size and type include prehistoric tools and implements, items dating from

the period of the Turkish occupation and memorabilia from the time of the 1848–9 War of Independence. Pride of place, however, (at least in Hungarian eyes) belongs to the exhibition of Hungarian Royal Regalia, including the 11th-century crown of St Stephen, presented by Pope Sylvester II. Note the crooked cross which appears on the Hungarian coat of arms, currently enjoying a revival.
Open: Tuesday to Sunday 10.00–17.00 hrs
Closed: Monday
Metro: Kálvin tér (line 3)

◆
MARGIT HÍD (MARGARET BRIDGE)
The original bridge, built to a French design from 1872 to 1876, was destroyed in 1944. It connects with the south end of Margit-sziget (Margaret Island).

◆◆
MARGIT-SZIGET (MARGARET ISLAND)
Rabbit Island as it was once known, was a Royal Game reserve at the time of the Árpád dynasty. It was for centuries the home of various monastic orders and tradition has it that Béla IV vowed during the Mongol invasion that he would bring his daughter up as a nun if his armies were victorious. Margaret, his daughter, was duly sent to the order of Dominican nuns which prospered under Béla's patronage. She was nine when she went to live on Rabbit Island and she stayed there until

Margaret Island: quiet gardens...

...and open-air theatre

she died in 1271. The island took her name at the end of the 19th century; she was canonised in 1943.

During the Turkish occupation many of the buildings on the island were destroyed; it then became the home of the nuns of St Clare and later passed into the hands of the Archduke Palatine Alexander. When Palatine Joseph took over the island in 1795 he planted it with vines and rare trees. In 1869 it was opened to the people as the public park –

accessible only by boat until 1900 when Margit híd (Margaret Bridge) was built. In 1908 the city bought the island and visitors were charged an entrance fee which doubled on Sundays and holidays. This kept the island rather exclusive until 1945 when it was declared a free public park for all citizens.

For the contemporary visitor it remains one of the most unspoilt and peaceful parts of Budapest, a haven for those seeking refuge from the hustle and bustle of urban life. Private cars can be driven on to the island only from

The Western Railway Station, an architectural sensation when it was built, and still formidable

the Árpád Bridge (built in 1950) and then only as far as the car park next to the Grand Hotel, but many parts of the island can be reached by bus or taxi. You can also hire cycles from here. Interesting places to visit include the Alfréd Hajós swimming pool (open to the public when no competitions on), the ruins of a Franciscan church and, on the east side of the island the ruins of the Dominican nunnery where St Margaret spent most of her life can be seen. St Michael's Church was built in 1930 using materials from the 12th century church of the nearby Premonstratensian convent; it boasts Hungary's oldest bell, dating from the 15th century, which was discovered under the roots of an upended tree in 1914. On the west side of the island are the Palantinus Baths, the island's chief attraction in summer. Several swimming pools of different temperatures, including one with artificial

ancient trees and overlooked by the Water Tower, built in 1911. The north end of the island (by the Árpád Bridge) contains the Grand Hotel and beyond is the modern Hotel Thermal; both hotels have a cosmopolitan flavour and are frequented by the wealthy. Near by is the peaceful and charming Japanese Water Garden. There is another open-air theatre used for performances by the Hungarian National Folk Ensemble near the Grand Hotel Car Park.

The Centennial Monument is near the Margaret Bridge access. This celebrates the hundredth anniversary of the coming together of Pest, Buda and Óbuda; it was erected in 1972 and designed by István Kiss. Behind it there is a fountain which is colourfully lit at night. In the centre of the island there are huge chestnuts, planes, oaks and acacia – many of them centuries old; willows and rare tulip trees are set on well-kept lawns. Lining the paths are busts of Hungary's most famous writers, artists and composers. János Arany, Hungary's great national poet (1817–1882) used to compose his verses in the shade of these ancient trees.
Bus: 26 from Nyugati tér
Cars: restricted access only

waves, are set in tree-studded parkland; single-sex terraces are set aside for sunbathing so it is quite proper to bare all and sunbathe in the nude. Margaret Island is said to be the inspiration for the magic garden in Wagner's opera *Parsifal* and the amphitheatre, with the capacity to seat 3,500 people, continues the island's operatic associations. It is the open-air theatre of the State Opera House and opera and ballet performances are staged throughout the summer. The vast stage is surrounded by

◆◆
MÚZEUM KÖRÚT AND BRÓDY SÁNDOR UTCA
As the name implies, the building dominating Múzeum körút is the neo-classical **Magyar Nemzeti Múzeum (Hungarian National Museum)** (see separate entry). On 15

The ultra-modern shopping complex, Skálá Metró at Nyugati tér

March 1848, the great poet, Sándor Petőfi, read out his 'National Song' from the top of the steps, an event which marked the beginning of the revolution of that year. The anniversary is now a public holiday and colourful celebrations take place outside. The monument in front of the museum commemorates another 19th-century poet, János Arany, and the adjoining garden contains more monuments to distinguished Hungarians, including Count Széchenyi and the poet/dramatist, Kisfaludy. **Bródy Sándor utca** is the street immediately to the left of the museum. The ornate yellow building at No. 7 is the former radio station from where, on 23 October 1956, secret police guards fired on protesters, initiating the Hungarian uprising. *Metro*: Astoria (line 2) or Kálvin tér (line 3)

◆◆
NÉPRAJZI MÚZEUM (ETHNOGRAPHICAL MUSEUM)
Kossuth Lajos tér 12
The sculptures of legislators, magistrates and goddesses of justice which adorn the façade of

over the world; items range from Eskimo furs and kayaks to carved Melanesian masks. Perhaps the most interesting displays are those illustrating the Hungarian peasants' way of life, culture and art. These displays are often supplemented by lively temporary exhibitions. Work tools, ornaments, costumes and 'room sets' all give the visitor a vivid picture.
Open: Tuesday to Sunday 10.00–18.00 hrs
Closed: Monday
Metro: Kossuth tér (line 2)

◆
NÉPSTADION
Stefánia út
Hungary's largest stadium was opened in 1953 and has a seating capacity of 76,000 spectators. It is now part of an extensive sports complex which includes a hotel, a sports museum and various stadia and sports halls.
Metro: Népstadion (line 2)

this late 19th-century building (its architect, Alajos Hauszmann) are explained by the fact that it was formerly the Palace of Justice. Inside it is no less imposing: the enormous entrance hall with marble stairways and huge chandeliers is the setting for a fine fresco by Károly Lotz (look up, it is on the ceiling) showing Justitia, the Goddess of Justice sitting on her throne among the clouds. By her side the groups of allegorical figures represent Justice and Peace (on her right) and Sin and Revenge (on her left). Permanent exhibitions here include a diverse collection of ethnological material from all

◆◆
NYUGATI TÉR AND TERÉZ KÖRÚT
One of the city's major traffic intersections, Nyugati tér (formerly Marx tér) is also the home of Budapest's most modernistic shopping complex, the Skála Aráház. Opposite is the handsome iron and glass façade of the Nyugati pályaudvar (Western Railway Station), built by the Eiffel company of Paris in the 1870s, before they went on to build the tower. On nearby Váci út is the glitzy Westend Shopping Center, selling non-stop hamburgers, jeans, sweatshirts etc.

*Statue of Ferenc Rákóczi II, an
18th-century freedom fighter*

Running east from Nyugati tér
are the stately Teréz körút and
Erzsébet körút. Nos 9–11, near
Dohány utca, is the **New York
Kávéház**. This was the favourite
haunt of Budapest's artistic set
and is well worth a visit. At the
height of its popularity in the
1910s and again in the late 1920s
and early 1930s, the café was
open 24 hours a day and
provided the writers who
patronised it (mainly on credit)
with free paper and ink. Journals
were edited here and
caricatures of the editors still
hang on the walls. It has been
restored to its original glory.

◆ ÖNTÖDEI MÚZEUM (FOUNDRY MUSEUM)

Bem József utca 20
On the site of the 19th-century
Ganz ironworks, which
produced the world's first
electric railway engine, the
museum contains a
reconstructed foundry and
workshop, as well as an
interesting collection of the
products once manufactured
here.
Open: daily 09.00–16.30 hrs
(Monday until 13.00 hrs)
Metro: Batthyány tér (line 2)

◆◆◆ ORSZÁGHÁZ (PARLIAMENT) ✓

Kossuth Lajos tér
For hundreds of years the
Hungarian National Assembly
had no permanent address.
When a new Parliament building
was projected back in the 1880s,
the then Prime Minister, Kálmán
Tisza, declared: 'There must be
no place for caution, calculation
and thrift.' Imre Steindl, the
architect, followed this directive
to the letter and produced an
edifice of genuine magnificence
which was, at the time of its
completion in 1902, the largest
and most lavish Parliament
building in the world. Work on
the building began in 1885;
Steindl died in 1902 a few weeks
before the building was
functioning.
Eclectic in style, but mainly

The Parliament building, from Buda

neo-Gothic in flavour (London's Palace of Westminster is an obvious source of inspiration), it stands guard over the Széchenyi embankment and the river running beneath. The height of the dome (315feet/96m) is an oblique reference to the foundation of the Magyar kingdom (AD 896) – **Szent István Bazilika (St Stephen's Basilica)**, which rises near by, is identical in height. Eighty-eight statues adorn the façade, which stretches for a total length of 869 feet (265m). There are nearly 700 rooms, approached by 27 entrances. Ninety pounds (41kg) of 24 carat gold were required for the gilding.

Of the 88 statues on the exterior, those on the Danube side are the Hungarian rulers, from the seven conquering chiefs to Ferdinand V, who died in 1848. On the Kossuth side are the princes of

St Stephen's Basilica

Food shop in Rákóczi út

Transylvania and several famous commanders; above the ground floor windows are the coats of arms of kings and princes. The main entrance leads to a vast ceremonial staircase which in turn leads to a 16-sided hall beneath the dome, used for official receptions and ceremonies. The National Assembly meets, several times a year, in the south wing which boasts an abundance of neo-Gothic ornamentation; as does the Congress Hall in the north wing (where the Upper House formerly met). Renovations began in 1925 and have not yet been finished.

Visitors should look out for some fine paintings, frescos, and tapestries by Mihály Munkácsy, Károly Lotz and Gyula Rudnay. Perhaps the most notable painting is Munkácsy's *The Magyar Conquest*, painted in 1893. To visit Parliament enquire at Tourinform (see Tourist Offices) as to visiting arrangements. Lajos Kossuth (1802–94), after whom Parliament Square is named, was a leading instigator of the 1848 revolution. A member of the council which ousted the monarchy and declared Hungary a republic, he was forced to flee the country when the Austrians regained control. He died in Turin but his body was brought back to Budapest, where his funeral was accompanied by three days of mourning.

Metro: Kossuth tér (line 2)

◆
PETŐFI HÍD (PETŐFI BRIDGE)
Named after Hungary's greatest poet, the revolutionary hero, Sándor Petőfi (1823–49), the bridge dates from the 1930s.

◆◆
RÁKÓCZI ÚT

One of the main shopping streets and with a less obviously Western orientation than some others, Rákóczi út runs from Múzeum Körút as far as Baross tér and the

Hungarian Television building

Keleti pályaudvar . Of the many famous Hungarians called Rákóczi, the one this street is named after was an 18th-century hero, Prince Ferenc Rákóczi II. The Verseny Áruház department store, one of the oldest in Budapest, stands at Rákóczi út 12. The **Dohány utca** (**Jewish**

Eastern Railway Station façade

District) (see entry) runs off to the left. The somewhat sleazy run of pizza bars, well-stocked clothes and electronic shops, bars and restaurants continues past the major intersection at Blaha Lujza tér where there is a metro station. At the end of Rákóczi út, on the left-hand side near the flyover, is the rather soulless Grand Hotel Hungaria. Much more impressive is the façade of the **Keleti pályaudvar (Eastern Railway Station)** (built 1881–4) which you can see ahead. On either side of the station entrance are statues of the British engineers George Stephenson and James Watt. *Metro*: Astoria or Keleti pályaudvar (line 2)

◆
SZABADSÁG HÍD (FREEDOM BRIDGE)

Another postwar reconstruction, this is on the site of an earlier bridge named after the Emperor Franz Josef.

◆◆◆
SZABADSÁG TÉR (FREEDOM SQUARE) ✓

Szabadság or Freedom Square is a vast open space in the centre of the city between **Országház (Parliament)** and **Szent István bazilika (St Stephen's Basilica)** (see entries). It was laid out by Antal Pálóczy in 1902. Three noteworthy buildings overlook the Square. On the west side is the former Stock Exchange, now **Hungarian Television Centre**. Opposite and dating from the same period (c 1905) is the **National Bank**. The attractive cream-coloured building with the wrought-iron balconies (on the corner of Perczel utca) is the **American Embassy**. The Hungarian Roman Catholic prelate, Cardinal Mindszenty, took refuge here during the 1956 uprising and was persuaded to

leave only 19 years later. In the centre of the square there is a small children's playground.

◆

SZÉCHENYI LÁNCHÍD (SZÉCHENYI CHAIN BRIDGE)

The most famous of Budapest's bridges was a wholly British venture, designed by an Englishman and built by a Scotsman, both coincidentally named Clark. The designer, William Tierney Clark, was also

responsible for Hammersmith Bridge in London. The first permanent link between Buda and Pest, the Chain Bridge was completed in 1849, against the wishes of the Austrians, who had tried to blow it up during the War of Independence!

◆
SZENT ISTVÁN BAZILIKA (ST STEPHEN'S BASILICA)

This monstrous edifice was designed by three architects, József Hild, Miklós Ybl and József Kauser, and completed in 1905 but only after the original dome had collapsed following a storm. It now serves as one of the city's major landmarks. The vast interior, which can hold more than 8,000 worshippers, is lavishly decorated with works of art by distinguished Hungarians, including Alajos Stróbl and

*Széchenyi Chain Bridge, a
famous Budapest landmark*

Károly Lotz, who designed the mosaics inside the dome. St Stephen's right hand is displayed in the Szent Jobb Kápolna (Chapel of the Holy Right Hand) behind the high altar.
Metro: Bajcsy-Zsilinszky út (line 1)

◆◆◆
SZÉPMŰVÉSZETI MÚZEUM (FINE ARTS MUSEUM) ✓

Hősök tere (Heroes' Square)
On the north side of Heroes' Square stands the Fine Arts Museum; a must for lovers of Western European art, it is one of the major galleries in Central Europe. The building was designed by Albert Schickedanz and Fölöp Herzog – also the architects of the Exhibition Hall (Műcsarnok) on the other side of the square (art exhibitions are displayed here).

The Fine Arts Museum is closed for renovation for one to two months each year (generally January, February or March); it is therefore impossible to describe the lay-out of the exhibitions, which are constantly on the move as dictated by the renovations, and you will have to explore as best you can.

Undoubtedly, the collection of Spanish School paintings is the jewel in the museum's crown. There are half a dozen El Grecos as well as works by Goya, Murillo and Veláquez. Other Old Masters worth hunting down in the galleries cover a representative collection of 13th- to 18th-century European painting and include works by Titian, Rembrandt, Raphael, Brueghel, Rubens, Van Dyck and Dürer. British painting is represented by works from Hogarth, Reynolds and Gainsborough. The core of the Old Masters collection came from Miklós Esterházy and was later added to by Károly Pulszky, a notable director of the museum. Pulszky, however, enraged the government of the day by his lack of interest in the work of contemporary Hungarian artists; he was dismissed and eventually committed suicide in Australia.

Strong on the French Impressionists and Post Impressionists, the modern foreign collection has, among others, works by Delacroix, Courbet, Millet, Gauguin, Monet, Renoir, Cézanne and Toulouse-Lautrec. Of the 20th-century artists, Picasso, Chagall, Kokoschka, Le Corbusier, and Vasarely are all represented. The museum has a vast holding of prints and drawings, which include works by Dürer, Rembrandt and Leonardo da Vinci. While the restoration work is in progress, a selection of these are periodically shown only in temporary displays. At present, most of the collection of European sculpture (mainly Italian and 17th- to 18th- century baroque work) is in storage; there are, however, some pieces displayed in various parts of the museum. Ancient Egyptian art is also represented here in a small but rich collection which includes painted wooden mummy cases, reliefs from the wall of a temple built during the 4th century BC and statuary. The Graeco-Roman

1920s chic: Don Cesar's pink hotel

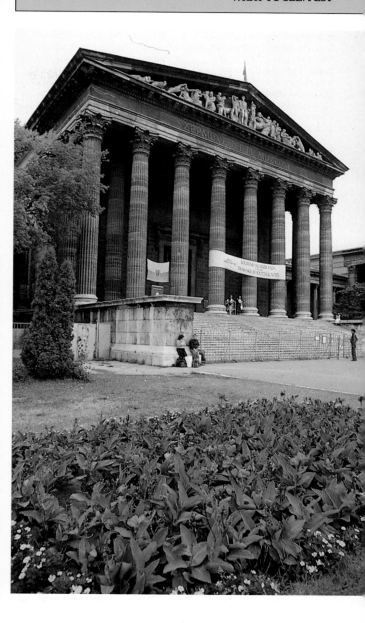

collection is of international importance and there are many fine examples of ceramics dating from the 6th to the 1st century BC.
Open: Tuesday to Sunday 10.00–18.00 hrs
Closed: Monday
Metro: Hősök tere

◆◆◆
VÁROSLIGET (CITY PARK)
City Park Area

Until the beginning of the 19th century this was nothing but a bare, open space. At the turn of the present century it was laid out as a park to complement the elegant new villas that were sprouting along Andrássy út. It is a popular resort for Pest dwellers even today – part wooded and partly given over to entertainments of a man-made nature. The City Park is the biggest of its kind in Budapest

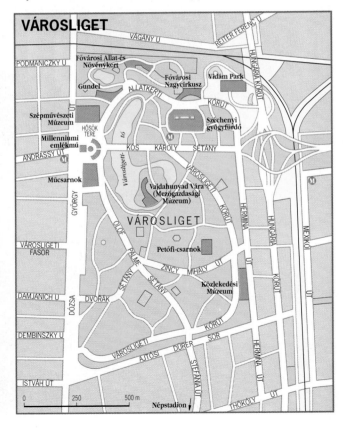

and was the chosen site for the great Millenary Exhibition in 1896, held to commemorate a thousand years of the Hungarian State. In all, over 200 halls and pavilions were erected and the country's first museum village was built to represent the lives of the peasants. Of course many of these buildings were dismantled after the exhibition was ended, but a few remain. Standing on an island in the boating lake is **Vajdahunyad Vár (Castle)** set amongst a group of trees. The castle was built for the exhibition. It was designed by the architect Ignác Alpár, and reflects a hotch-potch of architectural styles: Romanesque, Gothic, Transitional and Renaissance-baroque. Part of the castle was modelled on a castle of the same name which stands near Hunedoara in Romania; the original has become a casualty of the Ceaucescu regime and has been left to fall into decline. In all, 22 buildings were used as models for Budapest's Vajdahunyad and perhaps surprisingly, given the variety of styles, it is pleasing to the eye, giving the impression of a fairy-tale castle. Opposite the main entrance is a statue of Anonymus, the first medieval Hungarian chronicler. The entrance to the **Mezőgazdasági Múzeum** (Agricultural Museum) is found in the baroque wing of the castle, with exhibits on agriculture, animal husbandry, wine production, forestry and fishing. (*Open*: daily except Monday 10.00–18.00 hrs.) As well as an open-air skating rink (in winter only) City Park

has a variety of other attractions and places to visit. The **Fővárosi Allat-és Növénykert (Municipal Zoological and Botanical Gardens)** opened in 1866. They were founded by a member of the Academy of Sciences, János Xantus, a natural scientist who spent a great deal of time in the United States. The zoo boasts some impressive examples of the city's Art Nouveau heritage, for example the main gate, which is supported by four stone elephants. (*Zoo open*: daily 09.00–18.00 hrs, until 16.00 hrs in winter.) Budapest Zoo, one of Central Europe's oldest, boasts an international reputation for the high fertility rate of its hippopotami (which do not usually breed well in captivity) – this is apparently due to the constant supply of thermal spring water.

Next to the zoo is the **Fővárosi Nagycirkusz (Municipal Circus)** enquire at Tourinform for details of performances). The first circus in Pest, the Hetz Theatre was built on the site of the Lutheran Church in Deák tér. A permanent circus was then built on the present-day site although the building which stands now dates only from the early 1970s. Beyond the circus is **Vidám Park** (amusement park); the traditional merry-go-round and the wooden switchback are pre-war. There are, however, plenty of more modern rides plus a small children's playground between the circus and the funfair. (*Open*: daily 10.00–20.00 hrs.)

The **Széchenyi gyógyfürdő (Baths)** are found opposite the

circus. They were opened in 1913 and enlarged in 1927 to incorporate an open-air swimming pool and medicinal pools fed by thermal springs. This is one of the largest buildings of its kind in Europe and visited by an astonishing two million people a year. The Medicinal Baths, which were designed by Győző Czigler and Ede Dvozsák between 1909 and 1913, has a huge Art Nouveau mosaic inside the dome of the building; all the fittings from the tiles on the floor to the light

Vajdahunyad Castle, in City Park

fixtures are perfect period pieces. The northern wing of the building, with its neo-baroque interior, was designed by Imre Francsek. Here you will find regular visitors playing chess on floating cork chessboards whilst they sit in the thermal pools; there is also a lively restaurant with a view of the thermal pools so you can sit and watch this spectacle. Opposite the entrance to the baths is a statue of engineer and geologist, Vilmost Zsigmond, who discovered the first medicinal springs in the park in 1877. Towards the southeast corner of the park at Városligeti körút 11 is the **Közlekedési Múzeum (Transport Museum)** (see entry) and near by is the charming Garden for the Blind, a small garden especially designed to be appreciated by those with impaired sight.

The Transport Museum's exhibition on the history of aviation is located at a different venue, also in City Park: Petőfi Hall was rebuilt in 1985 on the site of an old exhibition hall and is now Budapest's main Youth Centre and the 'stronghold' of Hungarian rock and pop music. It is also the venue for a flea market, theatrical performances for children, a roller-skating club and a popular disco on Saturday evenings.

The statue of George Washington located in the park was funded by the Hungarian immigrants who arrived in the United States between 1871 and 1913.

◆◆
VÁSÁRCSARNOK (CENTRAL MARKET HALL)
Fővam tér

This vast neo-Gothic hall at the Pest end of the Szabadság hid (Freedom Bridge) was completed in 1896, and is now a protected monument. It has long been the city's favourite market and has recently reopened following reconstruction. Fruit, vegetables, meat and fish predominate but you can also buy artwork and handicrafts.
Open: Monday to Thursday 06.00–16.00 hrs, to 19.00 hrs Friday, to 15.00 hrs Saturday.
Closed: Sunday.
Metro: Kálvin tér.

◆
VIGADÓ TÉR to ROOSEVELT TÉR
This part of downtown Budapest is largely a late 19th-century development. The central feature of Vigadó tér is the **Vigadó kulturkozpunt (Concert Hall)**, designed in the 1860s by Frigyes Feszl. The richly decorated exterior gives the building its distinguished look, but the interior foyer, staircase and halls are more pleasing to the eye. (The frescos have recently been restored.) Liszt, Wagner and Mahler are among those who have performed here. **Roosevelt tér** was named after the US President, F D Roosevelt, in 1947. On either side of the square are monuments to the 19th-century statesmen, Ferenc Deák, author of the famous Compromise of 1867, and Count István Széchenyi (1791–1860), one-time Minister of Transport and a leading social and economic reformer. At the northern end of Roosevelt tér is the **Magyar Tudományos Akadémia (Hungarian Academy of**

Sciences), designed by the German architect, F A Stüler. *Metro*: Vörösmarty tér (line 1)

◆◆◆
VÖRÖSMARTY TÉR
and VÁCI UTCA ✓

This charming and restful square (now pedestrianised) is named after the 19th-century Romantic poet, Mihály Vörösmarty (1800–55), whose monument stands in the centre. On the north side, at No. 7, is the famous **Gerbeaud pastry shop**, named after the Swiss, Emil Gerbeaud, who took it over in 1884. At No. 2, La Boutique Suisse sells Swiss watches. **Váci utca**, on the far side of the square, is Budapest's most exclusive shopping street. A mecca for Westerners, the shops here are stocked with all the familiar brand names you thought you had left behind – Estée Lauder, Adidas, etc. There is a McDonalds of course at Nos. 94–8 (a favourite haunt of buskers in the evening) and a rival City Grill at No. 20. There is a pizza parlour and a whole range of electronic shops selling video equipment and even computers. Look out for the graffiti advertising Pet Shop Boys (sic), Beastie Boys, Sex Pistols etc.

◆
ZSIDÓ MÚZEUM (JEWISH MUSEUM)
Dohány utca 2
Located in the annexe of the Central Synagogue, in the heart of the Jewish district, the

Monument to Mihály Vörösmarty

museum traces the history of
Hungarian Jewry.
Open: April to October, Monday
to Saturday 10.00–14.00 hrs,
Sunday 10.00–13.00 hrs.
Metro: Astoria (line 2)

Around Budapest

BUDAI-HEGYSÉG (THE BUDA HILLS)

At some point in your stay you
will probably feel the need to get
away from the fumes and fury of
the city. Fortunately, the outskirts
of Budapest, especially the
woodland to the west, around
Szabadság-hegy (Liberty Hill),
have much to offer.
The easiest point of access is via
the cogwheel railway which runs
from Szilágyi Erzsébet fasor,
near the Hotel Budapest (bus 22
from Moszkva tér) to Albert utca.
Here you can pick up the
Pioneer Railway, seven and a
half miles (11km) of narrow-
gauge track, maintained and
administered by smartly
uniformed members of the
Hungarian youth movement who
do everything except drive the
trains. There are a number of
stops along the route: each has
its own attractions, from
secluded footpaths and
breathtaking views to wayside
restaurants and picnic areas. In
the winter, you can ski down the
slopes of **János-hegy**; the ski lift
continues to operate in the
summer, taking visitors on a
leisurely journey to the summit at
1,735ft (529m) from Zugligeti út.
If you want to stray beyond the
confines of the railway, buses
leave from various points in the
centre of town to a host of scenic

destinations, including
Hármashatár-hegy where, from
April to the end of October, you
can explore the fascinating
Pálvölgy and Szemlőhegy
stalactite caves. (Buses 65 and 29
respectively run from Kolosy tér,
halfway between the Árpád and
Margit Bridges. Or you can drive
from Kolosy tér along Szép-
völgyi út to the summit.)

THE DANUBE BEND (ESZTERGOM, SZENTENDRE, VISEGRÁD)

About 30 miles (50km) north of
Budapest, the River Danube
abruptly changes course
meandering south through a
beautiful stretch of hilly, unspoilt
countryside. The towns of the
Danube Bend are easily
accessible and well worth visiting.

Esztergom

Historic Esztergom had been the
centre of Hungary's Roman
Catholic church since the 11th
century. Appropriately the
Basilica, which dominates Castle
Hill, is the largest church in the
country. Little remains of the
original medieval building,
however, and the present
structure (designed by József
Hild) dates only from the early
19th century. The interior is
sumptuous but the main point of
interest is the Bakócz Chapel,
named after the cardinal who
commissioned it in the early 16th
century. When the old cathedral
was demolished the chapel was
reassembled, stone by stone, in
its present position. The altar, in
white marble, is the work of
Florentine craftsmen and was
designed by Andrea Ferrucci in

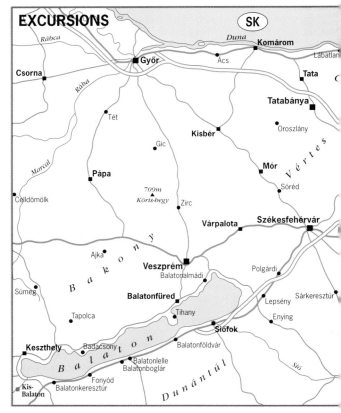

1519. Separate tickets are required to visit the crypt (the burial place of Esztergom's archbishops), the treasury, with its notable collection of precious objects, and the bell-tower from which there is a fine view of the Danube and the Pilis Hills. Before leaving Castle Hill take a few moments to inspect the reconstructed section of the **Vármúzeum (Medieval Royal Castle)** vacated when the court moved to Buda after the Mongol invasion. Your main ports of call should be St Stephen's Hall, the Hall of Virtues, decorated with Renaissance wall paintings, and the 12th-century chapel, with its distinctive rose window above the doorway.

On the far side of Bajcsy-Zsilinszky út is the Primate's Palace which houses the **Christian Museum**, a must for art lovers with its collection of old

Italian masters including works by Duccio, Lorenzo di Credi and Giovanni di Paolo. There are also some outstanding Hungarian and Bohemian altarpieces. Next door is the **Öreg-templon (Water Town Parish Church)**, which dates from the 18th century. Architecturally, Esztergom is a pot-pourri of styles and a stroll through the Watertown district in the direction of Széchenyi tér and the 18th-century Town Hall will

introduce you to baroque, rococo and classical (and the various staging posts in between!).
HÉV suburban railway: from Nyugati pályaudvar
Bus: from Erzsébet tér (Engels tér)
Boats: from Vigadó tér
Cars: Road 10 or the more scenic Road 11

Szentendre

Szentendre (St Andrew), a treat for tourists, with its delightful architecture and relaxed cultural atmosphere, is a mere 12 miles (18km) from Budapest. **Fő tér** is the focal point of the town. The ornate wrought-iron cross in the centre of the square was erected by Serbian merchants to commemorate deliverance from the plague in 1763. The Serbs, who began arriving as refugees from Ottoman Turkey as early as the 14th century, came to form a sizeable community in Szentendre. They built the **Blagoveštenska (Annunction) Church** and the four merchant houses dating from 1720–30, which now constitute the **Picture Gallery**. Paintings, tapestries and sculptures by members of the talented **Ferenczy** family can be found at No. 6 Fő tér, while, just around the corner, the **Margit Kovács museum** is devoted to a collection of her exquisite modern ceramics.
(*Open:* daily 09.00–17.00 hrs)
From Fő tér prepare yourself for a steep climb up **Castle Hill**, where you will find two more churches (Serbian Orthodox and Roman Catholic) and another small gallery dedicated to the works of the Impressionist, **Béla Czóbel**. Tourist Information is at

Dumsta J utca 22 (tel: 26/317-965).

About 2½ miles (4km) west of the town (catch a bus from the HÉV terminal on Dunakanyar körut, stand 8) is the open air **Szabadtéri Néprajzi Múzeum (Village Museum)**, an ambitious attempt to evoke the atmosphere of a 19th-century rural community. White-washed peasant houses, thatched roofs, wooden towers, churches, barns, mills have been moved here from all over Hungary.
Open: April–October 09.00–17.00 hrs
Closed: Monday
HÉV suburban railway: from Nyugati pályaudvar
Bus: from Erzsébet tér
Boat: from Vigadó tér
Cars: Road 11

Visegrád

One of the most picturesque spots on the entire Danube Bend, Visegrád is popular with Hungarians and foreigners alike. The Romans built the first fortified settlement here in the 4th century AD and it was still in use as late as the 10th century. At that time, Visegrád was inhabited by Slavs who gave it its present name, meaning 'lofty fortress'. Work began on the Royal Palace in the 13th century, and a succession of rulers added their own embellishments until King Matthias Corvinus had created what Pope Sixtus IV described as a 'Paradise on the earth'. Decline set in after the Turkish occupation and today Visegrád is once more a charming, but sleepy, backwater. The tourist route begins at Fő utca, near the

landing stage, where there is also a tourist office. So much of the **Palace** was destroyed that doubts were even expressed about its site until excavations began in 1934. They have been going on ever since. At the centre of the ruins, approached by a reconstruction of the original Gothic arcaded passageway, is the court of honour featuring a pilastered loggia and part of a Renaissance fountain – all that survives of the original palace built by Charles Robert of Anjou early in the 14th century. Near the outer wall, on the terrace, is a copy of the ornate Lion Fountain. The remains of the original can be seen in the **Solomon Tower**, the former keep of the lower castle, situated to the north of the

Bathing at Lake Balaton

landing stage. Built originally in the 13th and 14th centuries, it is now a **museum** containing various artefacts recovered from the Palace interior – the Hercules Fountain, being the most celebrated. A steep climb will take you to the **Fellegvár Citadel,** a superb vantage point for views and photographs.
Coach: from Nyugati pályaudvar
HEV suburban railway: to Nagymaros, onward by ferry
Bus: from Erzsébet tér
Boat: from Vigadó tér
Cars: Road 11 via Szentendre

◆◆
LAKE BALATON
*Approx 60 miles (100km)
southwest of Budapest*
Hungary's 'seaside' is actually the largest freshwater lake in Western Europe, with a shoreline of more than 125 miles (200km) and an area of 230 square miles (595sq km). All tastes are catered for here: sports enthusiasts will enjoy swimming in temperatures approaching 30°C (86°F) at the height of the summer and there are facilities for windsurfing, fishing (there are over 40 species of fish in the lake), sailing and cycling. Or you can lie out in the sun and relax on one of the sandy beaches along the southern shore. Resorts jostle for space around the perimeter of the lake offering shops, restaurants, bars and even a nightlife of sorts (though, surprisingly, discos tend to be few and far between).

The northern shore is the more attractive: **Balatonalmádi** (brash and modern with good facilities), **Balatonfüred** (spas, sanatoria and a busy harbour), **Tihany** (rich in history but over-popular), **Badacsony** (striking scenery) and **Keszthely** (bars and restaurants) are the main resorts. **Siófok**, the largest town on the southern shore, is the starting point for local excursions (tourist information: Fő utca 41, tel: 84/310-117).

Train: all destinations from the Southern Railway Station (Déli pályaudvar)

Cars: Motorway M7 or Highway 70 or 71 (southwest of city)

◆◆
ÓBUDA (OLD BUDA)

The Árpád Bridge crosses the southern tip of Óbuda Island.

The Basilica at Esztergom

Most of old Óbuda has been demolished to make way for housing estates and modern tower blocks; there are, however, several worthwhile art galleries and enough architecture to give the visitor an idea of its 'turn of the century' atmosphere. Indeed until the Tartar invasions it was the more important of the Buda settlements and only lost its prominence when Béla IV was compelled to flee behind the fortifications on Castle Hill in the mid-13th century. From this time it became known as Old Buda or Óbuda but still retained its royal patronage. The palace, built by Andrew II at the beginning of the 13th century, continued to be occupied by the queens or the royal dowagers under the Angevins; little remains of it now. Virtually nothing remains from the medieval settlements of Óbuda either, but

there are remains of its 18th- and 19th-century life. For example, the **parish church**, built by the local landlords, the Zichy family, in the 1740s has some fine sculptures mainly by Károly Bebó. The restored neo-classical synagogue (in Lajos utca) dates from 1821 and is now a cultural centre; it used to be surrounded by a Jewish ghetto but that has been pulled down.

In the **Fő tér (Main Square)** and surrounding streets there are several fine baroque houses; the area has been carefully restored. Zichy Mansion, completed in 1757, on the east side of the square, is the district's **cultural centre** and **Pince Gallery**. Its large internal courtyard is used for summer concerts and inside there is a collection of works by painter and writer **Lajos Kassák** (*open*: daily except Monday 10.00–18.00 hrs). The Óbuda **Local History Collection** is also housed here and this includes a display of barrel-making instruments. (*Open*: Tuesday to Friday 14.00–18.00 hrs, Saturday and Sunday 10.00–18.00 hrs).

On Szentlélek tér is the **Vasarély Museum**. Victor Vasarély, the founder of Op-Art, donated 400 of his works to the country of his birth. This museum displays a representative selection of his paintings and in addition features a library, lecture hall and often temporary exhibitions of one kind or another.
(*Open*: daily except Monday 10.00–18.00 hrs)

In the northeast corner of Fő tér there is the sculpture 'Strollers in the Rain'. The full-size bronze figures of women with umbrellas are the work of Imre Varga, one

of the most prolific of contemporary sculptors. More of his work can be seen at the nearby **Imre Varga Collection** at 7 Laktanya utca.

Another collection to visit in Óbuda is the **Zsigmond Kun Collection** at 4 Fő tér. Zsigmond Kun was a connoisseur and collector of ceramics and folk art; his former home is now a museum and the displays include pottery, textiles, carvings and furniture from all over Hungary. (*Open*: Tuesday to Sunday 10.00–18.00 hrs. *Closed*: Monday)

The **Kiscelli Museum** at Kiscelli utca 108 (formerly a Trinitarian Monastery and set on a wooded hill above the town) houses the modern department of the Budapest History Museum. There is a noteworthy collection of 20th-century pictures here but the museum also illustrates the capital's history from the liberation of the city from the Turks (1686) to the present day.
Open: Tuesday to Sunday 10.00–18.00 hrs.
Closed: Monday.
Bus: 86 to Flórián tér
HÉV suburban train: from Batthyány tér to Aquincum

Aquincum

Spread across the Óbuda area is the Roman site of Aquincum. The Romans settled here in the 2nd and 3rd centuries AD and at its zenith the population of Aquincum numbered around 40,000. At first it was mainly a Roman garrison town (about 6,000 soldiers were stationed here); later, as people from all parts of the Empire settled here, it became the provincial capital of Pannonia Inferior.

The military population lived in the area of what is today the town of Óbuda, the civilian population 2 miles (3km) to the north, so the remains are somewhat spread out. The general consensus is that it is best to begin a visit to the Roman remains with the ruins of the **Amfiteátrum (Military Amphitheatre)**. These are located at the corner of Nagyszombat utca and Pacsirtamező utca (about half a mile (1km) away from the Flórián tér; buses 6, 84 and 86). The amphitheatre, built in the 2nd century AD had the largest arena north of the Mediterranean capable of seating around 15,000 spectators who would flock to see the lavish, and sometimes bloody, spectacles. In the 4th century the amphitheatre was converted into a fortress; the evidence suggests that from then on battles constantly arose over its ownership. The ruins were discovered in 1937 and excavated until 1940.

The remains of a large villa on Meggyfa utca was probably once the home of a wealthy Imperial official. It is known as the **Herkules-villa** because of its well-preserved mosaic floors, dated to around the beginning of the 3rd century and depicting scenes from the legends of Hercules and Dionysus. These mosaics are among the best Roman remains in Hungary. (*Open:* May to October by appointment only, tel: 180-4650) The **Military Baths Museum** (*Open*: May to August by appointment only, tel: 180-4650) has an entrance in the underpass to Flórián tér and indeed the

underpass network beneath the square has become a **Roman Camp Museum** with display cabinets and stone remains lining the walls (*Open*: May to October, Tuesday to Friday 10.00–14.00 hrs, weekends 10.00–18.00 hrs.)

East of Szentendrei út (approx two and a half miles (4km) north of Flórián tér) is the site of the remains of the **walled civilian town** and the **Aquincum Museum** (*open*: May to October 10.00–18.00 hrs; *closed*: Monday). The museum was built in 1894 in neo-classical style to house Roman relics found in the area; its prize exhibit is a rare example of a 3rd-century organ. The remains of a civilian town are set around the museum and a good idea of its layout can be gained. The excavations include the remains of some large public baths, a market place, a temple, a shrine to the Persian sun-god Mithras, dwelling houses and a Christian church. Elsewhere in the area are the ruins of the **civilian amphitheatre**, far smaller than the military amphitheatre with a capacity for only 6,000.

Buses: 42 and 34 from Korvin Ottó tér (Szentlélek tér).

HÉV suburban railway from Batthyány tér, Buda to Aquincum station.

About half a mile (1km) from the Aquincum Museum there is the Római Outdoor Swimming Pool and Camping-Site (there is also a motel here). Lukewarm spring water – used for bathing by the Romans – feeds the swimming pools in one of the loveliest outdoor bathing areas of the city, set in open fields.

PEACE AND QUIET

Countryside and Wildlife in and around Budapest

by Paul Sterry

Whether you have an interest in natural history, or simply enjoy the peace and quiet of forests, lakesides or the countryside as a whole, Hungary has a great deal to offer. There are plenty of sites within easy access of Budapest itself for quiet contemplation or relaxed birdwatching.

Hungary is a landlocked country, bordered to the north by Slovakia and the Ukraine, to the west by Austria, to the south by Slovenia, Croatia and Yugoslavia and to the east by Romania. Within its comparatively small area (327 miles (526km) wide and 166 miles (268km) across) are flat, fertile plains, extensive lakes, forests, hills and mountains. Much of lowland Hungary is agricultural land, and the country is famous for its fruit and vegetable production. This land-use has all but eliminated the natural grassland landscape that once comprised the Alföld (Great Hungarian Plain) to the south and east of Budapest. However, here and there pockets of this habitat remain and many of the creatures associated with it manage to survive in the modern, man-made agricultural landscape.

In and Around Budapest

To get the most from a visit, it is probably best to hire a car and explore the country at a slow pace. However, those visitors on a short visit to the capital can still find plenty of wildlife interest near by. There are parks and gardens with interesting birds in the middle of Budapest and forests and hills lie on the outskirts. The following are some of the more interesting sites for visitors seeking peace and quiet and with an interest in natural history.

Margit-sziget (Margaret Island)

Except for the point of access on

PEACE AND QUIET

Margaret Bridge this haven of tranquillity is cut off from the city by the waters of the Danube. Private cars are banned from the area and the woodlands are a haven for birds such as woodpeckers and flycatchers. The island is an extremely popular recreational area, with swimming pools, sports grounds and gardens.

Városliget (City Park)

This park lies to the east of Hősök tere on the east side of the Danube in Pest. The central feature is a replica of Vajdahunyad Castle, surrounded by a man-made moat; there is also a zoo, agricultural museum, transport museum, amusement park, circus and baths. For birdwatchers, the spring and summer months are best in the extensive woodlands here. As with other parks in the city, best results are had by arriving early in the morning and by avoiding weekends and public holidays.

Budai-hegység (Buda Hills)

The Buda Hills fringe the western border of Buda and are a delightful area for relaxing strolls in woodland or for birdwatching; they can be reached on bus 65 from Ujlaki Parish Church. Three hills – Hill of the Three Boundaries, St John's Hill and Freedom Hill – dominate the area and there are trails and short ski lifts to allow exploration. Woodland birds, including birds of prey, warblers and woodpeckers, abound. Colourful flowers can be found in bloom in spring and summer while in autumn the woods are renowned for the variety and abundance of fungi they harbour. Visitors may

also wish to see the **Budakeski Game Park** (bus 22 to Korayi Sanatorium), where wild boar and deer are kept.

Birds of Budapest's Woodlands

Although the birdlife of the woods can be rather uninteresting in the winter, in spring the resident birds start singing, their numbers boosted by migrant visitors. Listen for the loud, fluty song of the golden oriole. Although males are bright yellow, they are difficult to spot in the dappled foliage and the song is the best clue to their presence. Several species of warblers also arrive in spring; the Bonelli's warbler has a high-pitched trilling song which is sung from high in the branches. Birds of prey circle over the more remote areas of woodland, scanning the ground below for food and advertising their territories. Look out for honey buzzards, which soar on broad, rounded wings that have conspicious bars on them.

Flycatchers

Flycatchers are summer visitors to the woods around Budapest. As their name suggests, these delightful birds catch insects, making aerial forays from a prominent perch. Two species are particularly common around the city. The collared flycatcher has black-and-white plumage with a prominent white collar. The red-breasted flycatcher has an orange-red breast and continually pumps its tail up and down.

Further Afield

Because Budapest is centrally placed in Hungary, many of the best wildlife areas, including national parks and reserves, can be reached in a day. The following are among the best sites.

Lake Velence
This shallow lake lies about 30 miles (48km) southwest of Budapest and is a popular holiday destination for residents of the capital. Migratory ducks and waders can be seen around the shores, and herons, egrets and warblers breed in the extensive reed-beds that fringe the margins. To reach Lake Velence, take Route 70 to Székesfehérvár – not the M7.

The red-breasted flycatcher

The road runs along the southern shores of the lake and visitors should stop at any suitable vantage points. Minor roads run along the eastern and western ends of the lake and fields and marshes should be searched for wading birds.

Lake Balaton
This huge lake lies southwest of Budapest. The quickest route from the capital is to take the M7; once there, roads run around the entire margin of the lake. Wetland birds can be seen in many undisturbed places around the lake, but the best site is probably the Kis-Balaton Reserve. This small, marshy lake lies between the villages of Vors,

PEACE AND QUIET

Zalavár and Balatonszentgyörgy at the western end of Lake Balaton. It boasts large numbers of breeding wetland birds and has an observation tower. To visit the reserve you need prior permission: contact the **Hungarian Nature Conservation Authority**, Budapest XII, Költő utca 21 (tel: 156-2133) or enquire at the tourist office in the town of Keszthely. The **Tihany peninsula**, which juts into the northern shores of Lake Balaton is a nature protection area. The volcanic scenery is largely wooded and there are marked trails.

Birds of the Lakes

Herons and egrets are the most conspicuous of Hungary's lakeland birds. Both little and great egrets breed in the country and can be identified by their all-white plumage. Little egrets have dark bills and black legs with yellow feet. The larger great egret has dark legs and feet and a yellow bill. Spoonbills are superficially similar to egrets: they are roughly the same size and have white plumage. However, they are easily told by their long, spatulate bills. Several species of herons are also found in Hungary's reed-beds and marshes. Most are rather secretive and require patient observation to see them.

Alföld (The Great Hungarian Plain)

The Great Hungarian Plain lies southeast of Budapest and is bordered to the west by the River Danube, to the north by mountains, and runs southeast to the Romanian and Yugoslavian

> ### White Stork
> The white stork is one of Europe's most familiar birds. It has a tall, heron-like stance and distinctive white plumage with black wings. The legs are reddish, as is the large, heavy bill. Storks often nest on buildings and are welcome visitors; they are considered to be a sign of good luck and a nesting stork confers good fortune on the household. White storks build large rather untidy nests of twigs and debris which are often used year after year. To induce the birds to nest, people often put old cartwheels or specially made wooden structures on their roofs to serve as bases upon which the birds can build. Storks are summer visitors to Hungary, arriving in April and departing in August and September to spend the winter in Africa

borders. Although much of the land between the Danube and the River Tisza to the east is cultivated, there are pockets of the natural steppe grassland left, together with salt lakes and woodlands, while beyond the Tisza the landscape is more unspoilt.

An introduction to the wildlife of the Great Hungarian Plain can be found less than 30 miles (48km) from the centre of Budapest. Take Route 50 southeast from the capital and turn off at Alsónémedi to the town of Ócsa. Here you will find wet meadows and alder carr woodland. Several species of waders breed in the meadows, including black-tailed godwits and redshank, and the woodland harbour rollers, golden orioles and red-footed falcons.

Continue along the road to

Szeged from the capital and you will find more birds characteristic of the plains. Just before you reach the town, stop to look at Lake Fehér-tó on the east side of the E75. Wildfowl and waders are often abundant here.

The Kiskunsági Nemzeti (National) Park comprises six separate areas of steppe land or 'puszta' to the east of Szeged. The administrative centre is at Kecskemét, while the best areas within the park are between Lakitelék and Töserdö on the Tisza, Fülöpszállás (a bird reserve) and the sand dune area between Bugac and Bocsa. There is a pastoral museum in Bugac and *csikósok* (cowboy) herding displays in Lajosmizse.

The Hortobágyi Plain

This is the largest remaining area of steppe grassland left in Hungary and lies between the River Tisza and the town of Debrecen to the east of Budapest. Part of the area is a national park, the headquarters of which are in the village of Hortobágyi. Hortobágyi is a birdwatcher's paradise, with something to see throughout the year: open country birds including great bustards and birds of prey are often seen and wetland birds breed around the ponds and lakes. Migration time is excellent with ducks, cranes and storks much in evidence. Use the minor roads to explore.

A white stork on its roof-top nest

PEACE AND QUIET

The threatened great bustard

Great Bustard

The Hungarian plains are among the best remaining areas for one of Europe's largest and most threatened birds – the great bustard. They have bulky bodies and long necks and legs and are found only in flat, open country. Males, which are larger than females, are Europe's heaviest bird. In flight they resemble a huge goose, while on the ground they have an upright stance. In the spring, males perform elaborate displays to attract females: they inflate their throats, pull back their necks and fan out white feathers in the tail and wings.

Gemenci-erdő (The Gemenc Forest)

This forest lies near the town of Baja, south from Budapest on Route 51. It is part of the Danube's floodplain, and is made up of a mosaic of wetlands, marshes and woodlands of different types. The best areas of woodland lie on the west bank of the Danube both to the north and the south of the town. Gemenc is an excellent area for woodland birds, wild boar and deer, but is well worth visiting for its beauty alone. Access to the forest reserve is controlled: visitors can either take boat tours or travel on the small-gauge railway.

Visegrád

Visegrád lies to the north of Budapest on the south bank of the Danube; it can be reached by taking Route 11 from the capital. The surrounding hills are covered in forests which are excellent for woodland birds, mammals, flowers and fungi. In the vicinity is the Pilis Park Forest, a former Royal hunting ground, which is also good for wildlife.

Bükki Nemzeti (National) Park

This national park lies on a limestone massif, northeast of Budapest, and has caves, waterfalls and gorges. The extensive forests of beech and oak have been untouched for many years and have exceptionally rich ground flora, including many species of orchids. Not surprisingly, the birdlife is rich and woodland mammals thrive. The administrative centre for the national park is in Miskolc; access to the region is either from Miskolc or from Eger. The most scenic route is along the mountain road between the two towns, which passes through Répáshuta and Bükk-szentkereszt.

FOOD AND DRINK

Food

Hungarian food is both rich and filling. It is also fairly heavily meat-based, so vegetarians can be in for a hard time, though you will find, apart from vegetables, some pulses and egg dishes (the word for egg is *tojás*). You should see some fish on most menus. The soup is often a meal in itself. *Gulyás* is chunks of beef with potatoes and vegetables thrown in. Drink it slowly because it is usually very heavily spiced with the ever present paprika. *Halászlé* is a hot fish soup. You may also find *Hortobágyi palacsinta* on the menu. These are pancakes filled with mincemeat and covered in sour cream. Vegetarians may like to look out for *körözött*, a specially prepared ewe's cheese, often served with butter, chives and paprika. For the main course, you are likely to be offered such things as *Balatoni fogas* (pike-perch from Lake Balaton), *fatányéros* (mixed grill), *töltött káposzta* (stuffed cabbage). If you are eating in a fairly suave establishment, you may be offered goose liver, venison, wild boar or other game. Main meals are served either with salad or potatoes. If you have any room left, try *meggyes* (sour cherry), *rétes* (strudel) or *palacsinta* (pancakes) with various fillings.

Drink

The most famous white wines are known collectively as *Tokaji* from the region in which they are grown. They come in sweet and dry varieties but tend to be a little on the heavy side. If you prefer red wine, try *Egri Bikavér* (bull's blood). The authentic Hungarian spirits are brandies called *pálinka*. There are various flavours: *barack* (apricot), *cseresznye* (cherry) and *szilva* (plum). Vermouth is *ürmös*. The best Hungarian beers are Kőbányai and Dreher, but you will also find Czech Urquell and a large number of foreign brands (Tuborg is very big here). If you are out and about and in need of a drink, the general name for beer is *sör* and for wine, *bor*. A wine bar is *borozó* and a beer bar, *söröző*. A half -litre of beer is a *korsó*.

Restaurants

There is no shortage of eating establishments in Budapest and, at the present rate of exchange, they are good value. Be adventurous and look about you while you are wandering around. There are many cheap and cheerful cafés and restaurants in the less fashionable areas of the city centre, for example along Fő utca. The common name for restaurant is either *étterem* or *vendéglő*. Menus are usually available in an eccentric English or German (sometimes French). Hungarians tend to make the mid-day meal their main meal. Look out for early closing – Hungarians tend to eat early and you will not find it easy to order a meal after 21.00 to 21.30. While credit cards are becoming more generally acceptable, you will be surprised at the number of places which still do not accept them, so come with plenty of cash.

Fashionable Gundel Restaurant

Alabárdos, Országház utca 2, Budapest I (tel: 156-0851). Excellent food and drink in a medieval atmosphere, but pricey. Booking essential. Closed Sunday.

Arany Hordó, Tárnok utca 16, Budapest I (tel: 156-6765). This restaurant, wine cellar and beer hall, in the heart of old Buda, dates from the 15th century. Open until midnight.

Astoria, Kossuth Lajos utca 19, Budapest V (tel: 117-3411). A Gösser beer bar which also sells very reasonably priced meals. Favoured by young Hungarians. Closes 01.00 hrs. **Dominican** and **Kalocsa** (Hilton Hotel), Hess András tér 1–3, Budapest (tel: 175-1000). The Dominican specialises in international and French dishes, while the Kalocsa offers a Hungarian menu. Gypsy music in the latter. Closes midnight.

favourite haunt of politicians, artists and diplomats, it is still fashionable. Hungarian cuisine, of course, and gypsy music. Booking, and jacket and tie essential. Closes midnight.
Japan, Luther utca 4–6, Budapest VIII (tel: 114-3427). Situated off Rákóczi út, this smart establishment specialises, as the name implies, in Japanese cuisine. Closes 23.00 hrs. **Margit Kert**, Margit utca 15, Budapest (tel: 135-4791). Located in the affluent Rózsadomb district (not far from the Margaret Bridge), the Margitkert is patronised by bingeing foreign tourists and wealthy Hungarians. The food is delicious and only moderately expensive but watch out for over-charging. Gypsy music with a western orientation. Booking essential. Major credit cards.

Mátyás Pince, Március 15 tér 7, Budapest V (tel: 266-8008). Much favoured by Hungarians, this centrally situated restaurant (near the Elizabeth Bridge) is decorated with scenes from the life of King Matthias Corvinus. Gypsy music a speciality.

Ménes Csárda, Apáczai Csere János utca 15, Budapest V (tel: 117-0803). This excellent restaurant is situated between the Forum Hotel and Váci utca. Typical Hungarian dishes are cooked at your table to the accompaniment of a cymbalom. Prices are reasonable.

Szecsuán, Márvány utca 19, Budapest XII (tel: 156-6363). As the name implies, a Chinese restaurant, which stays open until 01.00 hrs on Friday and Saturday. Closed Sunday.

Dunacorso Vigadó tér 3, Budapest V (tel: 118-0913). Eat out on the terrace in the summer and you will have a fine view across the Danube to Buda. Cheap and cheerful.

Gundel, Állatkerti Körút 2, Városliget (City Park), Budapest XIV (tel: 121-3550). One of the most famous eating establishments in Budapest, it takes its name from Károly Gundel, who became the owner in 1910. Formerly a

FOOD AND DRINK

Tabáni Kakas, Attila út 27,
Budapest I (tel: 175-7165). An
intimate restaurant at the foot of
Castle Hill. Open until
midnight.
Trombitás, Retek utca 12,
Budapest II (tel: 135-1374). A
smart Hungarian restaurant
which stays open late.

The Danube Bend
Aranysárkány, Alkotmány utca
1–2, Szentendre (tel: 26/311-
670). French and Hungarian
cuisine at affordable prices.
Alabárdos, Bajcsy-Zsilinsky
utca 49, Esztergom (tel: 33/312-
640). A garden restaurant
serving lunch and evening
meals at very reasonable
prices.
Sirály Étterem, Rév utca 7 (tel:
26/328-376), Visegrád. Music is
the special feature here.
Traditional Hungarian food.

Cafés and Pastry Shops
Gerbeaud, Vörösmarty tér 7,
Budapest V (tel: 118-1311).
This famous pastry shop dates
from 1858 but takes its name
from the Swiss, Emil
Gerbeaud, who took it over in
1884. Very crowded but the
cakes are delicious!
Korona, Dísz tér 16, Budapest I
(tel: 175-6139). A pleasant
place to break from a
morning's sightseeing in Buda.
Lukács, Andrássy út
(Népköztársaság útja) 70,
Budapest VI (tel: 1321-371).
Situated opposite the Puppet
Theatre on the way to Kodály
körönd, this café dates back
from the turn of the century,
when it was founded by Sándor
Lukács. Specialises in pastries
and ice cream.

*The New York café – pre-war haunt
of intellectuals. Now it's pricey*

New York, Erzsébet körút
9–11, Budapest VII (tel: 122-
3849). Known as the New York
before World War II, when it
was frequented by artists and
writers, it is worth sampling for
its historical associations, but
you won't find it cheap. Open
09.00–midnight daily.
Ruszwurm, Szentháromság tér
7, Budapest I (tel: 175-5284).
Just across the street from the
Matthias Church, this
renowned pastry shop has

been here since 1827. Come early or be prepared to queue.

Fast Food
In and around Váci utca:
McDonalds (entrance in Régiposta utca) is now well established but long queues can form. The same may be true at the nearby City Grill. If so, there's a Pizzeria in Váci utca. The International Trade Centre has a number of cafés and restaurants including the City Grill.
In and around Nyugati tér:
The West End Shopping Center, behind the Western Station, has a number of fast food service points. You will find more on nearby Teréz körút.

There is also plenty of fast food on sale at the western end of Rákóczi út between Blaha Lujza, tér and the Astoria.

If you want something Hungarian, call in at a bar or *Étterem* (restaurant) or one of the new 'Paprika' fast food restaurants at Szt István körut 5, Harmincad ut 4, Pilvax kõz 1–3 or Oktober 6 ut 6 (all in district 5).

SHOPPING

Budapest is by Eastern-bloc
standards an extremely
consumer-orientated city. You
will find a wide variety of stores:
many of them organised along
Western lines.

The price of **food** has risen
astronomically. Supermarkets are
the most accessible (and often
the cheapest) places to buy
food. They also offer souvenirs
to take home, like Hungarian
wine and tins of paprika. Fruit
and vegetables, which are still
relatively cheap, are sold from
stalls throughout the city, but it is
better to go to the Vásárcsarnok
on Fővám tér, Budapest's main

Vörösmarty tér craft stalls

market hall. Here you will find a rich variety of fruit and vegetables and festoons of scarlet paprika strung up over the trader's stalls (open Monday to Thursday 06.00–16.00 hrs, Friday to 19.00 hrs, Saturday to 15.00 hrs). Other markets are held at Bosnyák tér, Budapest XIV, Lehel tér, Budapest XIII (which is also open on Sunday morning) and a flea market known as the Esceri, claimed to be the biggest in Eastern Europe, at Nagykőrösi út, Budapest XIX (open Monday to Friday 08.00–16.00 hrs, Saturday 08.00–15.00 hrs), which sells just about everything in the bric-à-brac line.

What to Buy
Clothes
These are often cheaper than they are in the West, although the gap is narrowing all the time. The department stores (*áruház*) on Rákóczi út might render up some stylish bargains.

Books
The book shop at Váci utca 32 is a popular one with tourists. It stocks a range of novels and coffee-table books by Hungarian authors published in foreign languages.

The best selection of **maps** can be found at Bajcsy Zsilinsky út 37, Budapest VI, or Nyár utca 1, Budapest VII. Both of these are outlets for the Cartographia company and, if you plan to travel to other former Eastern bloc countries, the maps here are better than anything available when you arrive.

Folk Art
Folk art is very popular in Hungary and provides the most characterful gifts or souvenirs of

your visit. Splendid carved and engraved wooden furniture is left in its natural colour; 'tulip chests' (trousseau chests) are painted with flower designs on a blue background. Smaller items include salt cellars and kitchen implements: these are made from wood, or sometimes horn, and adorned with figures from folk tales. Aside from these there are hand-woven and hand-embroidered shirts; the beautiful embroidered patterns include the simple black and white designs of southeastern Hungary and Transdanubia Mezőkövesd. Hand-woven and embroidered pillows, tablecloths and curtains (often seen in the parlours of local homes), coats and jackets, hand-knotted rugs and bone lace are also sold to tourists. Hungary's most famous **porcelain** is Herend china, noted for its hand-painted folk flower motifs and extremely expensive to buy in the West. But modern folk pottery, made from terracotta or the 'black' vases from Nádudvar, colourfully painted plates, dishes and jugs and bokály jug-like vessels (with no pouring lip) are equally tempting purchases. The best place to buy genuine Hungarian-made items is in one of the "Folkart" shops, where items carry a state-approved label of authenticity. The biggest and best branch, Folkart Centrum, is at Vaci utca, 14. Here you can also pick up a list of their branches around town. Craft items are also sold at the stalls which crowd Vörösmarty tér and the Corso on weekends. Szentendre is

SHOPPING

Váci utca – for smart shopping

another place where you will be
spoiled for choice by itinerant
sellers.

Flea Market

There is a Flea market on
Saturdays and Sundays (09.00 to
14.00 hrs) on Petőfi Csarnok,
which is a good place to view
and buy decorative folk art.
Other shops selling folk art and
crafts include those at:
Margit körút 34, Budapest II
Váci utca 14, Budapest V
Kálvin tér 5, Budapest V
Teréz körút 26, Budapest VI
Erzsébet körút 5, Budapest VII
Rákóczi út 32, Budapest VII
Jósef körút 78, Budapest VII
Bartók Bela út 50, Budapest XI
Szent István körút 26, Budapest
XIII

Antiques

These can be a good buy in
Hungary, although you won't
necessarily find many bargains.
The state-owned chain
Bizományi Áruház Vállalat (BAV)
is the best bet with branches at:
Ferenciek tere 3, Budapest V;
Szent István körút 3, Budapest V;
Andrássy út 27, Budapest VI.

Upmarket shops

In the Váci utca and
neighbouring streets you will

and department stores known as
áruház. Other shops are often
known by the names of what
they sell and do not have names
as we know them in the West. It
is worth taking Hungarian and
foreign currency with you when
you shop – credit cards are not
widely accepted.

Saturday is not a good day to
shop: the supermarkets are
crowded and many of the
smaller shops are shut after
13.00 hrs. One thing that
Budapest does still have in
common with the other former
Eastern bloc countries at the
moment is its system of making
purchases in the larger non-food
stores. The procedure is to
select what you want to buy;
collect a bill; pay at a separate
till and then return to the counter
and collect the goods, however
this is now being phased out.
VAT, charged at 25 per cent, is
included in the price of most
goods and services.

Food can be bought at the
Skála Csarnok in Klauzál tér
from 07.00–20.00 hrs
(Wednesday until 15.00 hrs);
closed on Sundays. See also
pages 88–9.

Opening hours

Department stores: Monday to
Wednesday, Friday 10.00–17.00
or 18.00 hrs, Thursday
10.00–20.00 hrs. Saturday 10.00
to 13.00 hrs. Sunday generally
closed.

Food shops: Monday to Friday
07.00 or 08.00–18.00 hrs,
Saturday 08.00–noon or 13.00 hrs.
On Sundays, shops are generally
closed, although it is quite easy
to find milk, bread, pastries, etc
from 06.00 to 14.00 hrs.

find the shops of Adidas, Estée
Lauder and La Boutique Suisse.
The International Trade Centre
is at Helia-D Váci út 19 (sells,
among other things, cosmetics).

Electrical items

For electrical goods go to Saba-
Revox on Párisi utca 19 6A.
There is a modern precinct
called Skálá Metro at Nyugati
tér, Budapest VI and the
following streets are also
commercial:
Kossuth Lajos utca, Rákóczi út,
Múzeum körút and Andrássy út.

Supermarkets

Most supermarkets are known
by their trade name, eg ABC,

ACCOMMODATION

Traditionally, because there simply has not been the demand, there has been a shortage of hotel accommodation in Hungary. Now, however, things have changed and in Budapest alone several new hotels have recently been constructed. A selection is listed below. Because of the general scarcity, it is advisable to book well in advance, especially in the summer.

Book through:

Danube Travel (IBUSZ), 6 Conduit Street, London W1R 9TG (tel: (0171) 493 6963)

Hungarian Travel Bureau

The Atrium Hyatt and the Forum Hotels

(North American Division), One Parker Plaza, Suite 1104, Fort Lee, N.J. 07024 (tel: 201 592 8585)

Hungarian Air Tours, Kent House, 87 Regent Street, London W1R 7HF (tel: (0171) 4379-405). Hungarian Hotels Sales Office, Suite 670, 6033 West Century Boulevard, Los Angeles, CA 90045 (tel: (310) 649–5960).

The Hungarian Tourist Board issues an annual list of accommodation in *Hotel Hungária*, obtainable from IBUSZ offices. The Tourinform office, Sütő utca 2, Budapest V (tel: 117-9800), are able to make accommodation reservations, for personal callers only (daily, 08.00–20.00 hrs). IBUSZ Hotel Service, Petőfi tér 3, Budapest V (tel: (118-

4842), run a 24-hour service for booking accommodation. Hotels are graded from 1 to 5-star. Bed and breakfast accommodation (pensions), private rooms in a family's home and some flats are also available through the booking agancies.

Outside Budapest, signs offering *szoba kiadó* or *zimmer* (rooms) will be seen along major roads. You can usually get a room here without making a reservation. Cheaper accommodation takes the form of hostels with dormitory-style bedrooms. Expressz Kozponti Iroda, Szabadság tér 16, Budapest V, (tel: 131-7777) has details of available beds. It is also possible to rent bungalows on campsites. See also **Camping** page 109, and

Student and Youth Travel
page 122.

Hotels–Budapest

Asoria Hotel, Kossuth Lajos utca 19, Budapest V (tel: 117-3411, fax: 118-6798), 3-star, 130 rooms. Fine fin-de-siècle building, gentlemen's club style bar. Handy for Metro and Váci utca.

Atrium Hyatt Hotel, Roosevelt tér 2, Budapest V (tel: 266-1234, fax: 266-8659), 5-star, 353 rooms. International hotel and conference centre overlooking Danube and Castle Hill.

Buda Penta, Krisztina-körút 41–3, Budapest I (tel: 156-6333, fax: 156-694) 4-star, 395 rooms. Nice situation, close to the castle.

Forum Hotel, Apáczai Csere János utca 12–14 Budapest V

ACCOMMODATION

(tel: 117-8088, fax:117-9808), 4-star, 400 rooms. Centrally situated with Danube views.
Gellért Hotel, Szent Gellért tér 1, Budapest XI (tel: 185-2200, fax: 166-6631), 4-star, 239 rooms. Traditional spa hotel, situated at the foot of Gellért Hill. Recently renovated, Art

The pool at the Gellért, a traditional spa hotel

Nouveau building of early 1900s.
Grand Hotel Corvinus Kempinski, Erzsébet tér 7–8 (tel: 266-1000, fax: 266-2000), 5-star, 368 rooms/suites including

ACCOMMODATION

2 presidential apartments. This is one of the most striking post-modern hotels in the city. Trade Centre opposite. Facilities for handicapped.

Grand Hotel Hungária, Rákóczi út 90, Budapest VII (tel: 122-9050, fax: 122-8029), 4-star, 528 rooms. A short walk from the Eastern Railway Station.

Hilton Hotel, Hess András tér 1–3, Budapest I (tel: 175-1000, fax: 156-0285), 5-star, 323 rooms. Building incorporates part of an abbey and a church. On a prime site in the heart of Buda.

Korona Hotel, Kecskeméti utca 14, Budapest V (tel: 117-4111, fax: 118-3867), 4-star, 433 rooms. In a prime position at Kálvin tér, opposite the National Museum.

Liget Hotel, Dózsa György út 106, Budapest VI (tel: 111-3205, fax: 131-7153), 3-star, 160 rooms. Overlooking the Fine Arts Museum and the Zoo in the City Park.

Metropol Hotel, Rákóczi út 58, Budapest VII (tel: 1421-175), 2-star, 100 rooms. Basic facilities in a busy downtown setting.

Raddison Béke, Terez Körút 43, Budapest VI (tel: 132-3300), 4-star, 238 rooms. On the boulevard ring, a short Metro ride from the city centre.

Ramada Grand Hotel, Margit-sziget, Budapest XIII (tel: 131-7769, fax: 153-3029), 4-star, 162 rooms. A beautiful setting on Margaret Island for this old spa hotel.

Park Hotel, Baross tér 10, Budapest VIII (tel: 113-1420) 2-star, 157 rooms. Basic facilities and centrally situated, close to the Eastern Railway Station.

Taverna Hotel, Váci utca 20, Budapest V (tel: 138-4999, fax: 118-7188), 3-star, 224 rooms. Part of an entertainment complex at the heart of the shopping district.

Thermal Hotel Margit-sziget, Budapest XIII (tel: 111-1000), 5-star, 206 rooms. A modern spa hotel, on the Margaret Island in the middle of the Danube.

Thermal Hotel Aquincum , Árpádfejedelem útja, Budapest III (tel: 188-6360, fax: 168-8872), 4-star, 312 rooms. A Hungarian – Swiss joint venture. Some rooms have views across to Margaret Island.

Thermal Hotel Helia, Kárpát utca 62–64, Budapest XIII (tel: 129-8650, fax: 120–1429), 4-star, 262 rooms and 8 suites. A Hungarian–Finnish joint venture, situated opposite the Thermal Hotel Aquincum (see above).

Hotels–Lake Balaton

Hotel Marina, Széchenyi utca 26, Balatonfüred (tel: 863 43 644), 3-star, 350 rooms.

Európa Hotel, Petőfi-sétány 17, Siófok (tel: 843 13 4 11), 3-star, 276 rooms.

Hotel Auróra, Bajcsy-Zsilinszky utca 14, Balatonalmádi (tel: 803 38 810), 3-star, 480 beds.

Hotels–Danube Bend

Hotel Esztergom, Primás sziget, Nagy-Duna sétány Esztergom (tel: 331-2833), 3-star, 36 rooms.

Hotel Ister, Ady Endre utca 28, Szentendre (tel: 26/312-497), 2-star, 48 rooms.

Hotel Silvanus, Fekete-hegy, Visegrád (tel: 26/398-170), 3-star, 69 rooms.

CULTURE ENTERTAINMENT, NIGHTLIFE

Budapest has a lively nightlife, catering for most tastes. Although many restaurants close at 23.00 hrs, you can sometimes get a meal later in the big hotels, especially at weekends. Concerts and theatre performances usually begin at 19.00 or 19.30 hrs. Nightclubs and discos are on the increase and some stay open as late as 04.00 or 05.00 hrs. The Metro, remember, closes down at around 23.00 hrs.

Music

In the field of classical Music, Budapest is as well served as any major city in the West, maintaining the strong tradition Hungary has always had of nurturing some of the world's greatest conductors, composers and performers. The city has two opera houses and three major concert halls. In the summer, some concert halls close but performances continue out of doors. You can hear grand opera or Hungarian folk music, for example, on Margaret Island's open-air stage or rock music at the Buda Youth and Leisure Centre. In the field of classical music, Bartók, Kodály and Liszt hold pride of place. The Spring and Autumn Festivals and Music Weeks are highlights of the year for concert-goers, and the State Opera is widely acclaimed at home and abroad.

Tourist information centres will have *Programme in Hungary*, and *Budapest Panoráma*, free monthly publications, listing all major cultural events. Look out too for wall-posters advertising special events.

Main concert halls

Academy of Music, Liszt Ferenc tér 8, Budapest VI (tel: 142-0179).
Budapest Convention Centre, Jagelló út, 1–3, Budapest XII (tel: 161-2869).
Pesti Vigadó, Vigadó tér 2, Budapest V (tel: 118-9903). The Central Booking Office (Központi Jegyirodaja), Vörösmarty tér 1, Budapest V (tel: 117-6222), is the place for advance tickets.

Opera and Operetta

State Opera House, Andrássy út 22, Budapest VI (tel: 153-0170).
Erkel Theatre, Köztársaság tér 30, Budapest VIII (tel: 133-0540).
Arany János Szinház, Paulay Ede út 35, Budapest VI (tel: 141-5626).

Musicals

West End and Broadway hits such as *Cats, Evita, Les Misérables* etc are regularly performed at a number of smaller theatres. For example:
Madách-Theatre, Erzsébet körút 29–33, Budapest VII (tel: 122-2015).
Művész-Theatre, Nagymező utca 22–4, Budapest VI (tel: 131-0500).
Operetta Theatre, Nagymező utca 17, Budapest VI (tel: 132-0535).

Gypsy music

It varies in degrees of authenticity, but it abounds in restaurants and cafés.

Traditional Hungarian music and dance

This can be seen on stage at the

Municipal Cultural Centre, Fehérvári út 47, Budapest XI (tel: 181-1360).

Theatre
Theatre tickets (programmes in Hungarian) can be obtained from: the Central Theatre Booking Office (Színházak Központi Jegyirodája), Andrássy út 18 (tel: 112-0000).

Cinema
Films are screened in English, French, German and Italian all over the city. See *The Budapest Sun* or *Budapest Week* for details.

Nightclubs (Floorshows)
Horoszkóp (Buda Penta Hotel), Krisztina körút 41–3, Budapest I (tel: 156-6333). *Open*: 22.00–04.00 hrs, show starts at 23.00 hrs.

Maxim Varieté (Emke Hotel), Akácfa utca 3, Budapest VII (tel: 122-7858). *Open*: daily except Sunday 20.00–01.00 hrs.
Star Night Club (Thermal Hotel Margit-sziget), Margit-sziget, Budapest XIII (tel: 111-1000). Non-stop Latin-American and disco music, open: 22.00 hrs to 03.00 hrs.

Discos
Discos abound in Budapest and new disco bars are opening all the time:
Hully Gully Lékai tér 9, Budapest XII (tel: 175-9742). *Open*: 21.00–05.00 hrs.
Petőfi Csarnock, Zichy Mihály

Live music is a strong tradition in Hungary

utca 14, Budapest XIV (tel: 142-4327). Saturdays.

Casino
The Budapest Casino is in the Hilton Hotel, Hess András tér 1–3 (tel: 175-1333). Offers roulette, baccarat, blackjack and video games. Hard currency only. Passports have to be shown. *Open:* 17.00 to 02.00 hrs.
Schönbrunn Casino, on a boat at the Pest end of the Chain Bridge (Lánchíd) Budapest V, (tel: 138-2016). Roulette, blackjack and video games. *Open:* May to October, 17.00–02.00 hrs.

WEATHER AND WHEN TO GO

Budapest is at its coldest in January, when the average temperature drops to –2°C (28°F). Spring often produces warm spells. In July, the average temperature rises to 22°C (72°F) but be prepared for much hotter weather 30°C plus (86°F). The humidity during August, especially in Budapest itself, can make sightseeing unpleasant but

theatre and opera performances are held in the open air to compensate. Hungary boasts over 2,000 hours of sunshine a year (higher than the average for Central Europe) and a visit during the milder spring or autumn months (when the Budapest Festivals are held) could be particularly rewarding.

HOW TO BE A LOCAL

On the face of it, a difficult proposition given the remoteness of the language. German is the preferred *lingua franca* – a reminder of Hungary's imperial past – but nowadays many young people have at least a smattering of English. Try to learn the Magyar words for good day, please and thank you (see **Language** below pp. 124–5). Even a token effort will win you friends. Wander off the beaten track as much as possible – buy the best local map the streets are well signposted and there is an efficient public transport system, so you are not likely to go far wrong. Drop in at a small bar or *étterem* (restaurant) and you will be eating and drinking in authentic surroundings.
The **Turkish baths** are a popular haunt for world-weary Hungarians, anxious to catch up on the gossip and if you are not totally daunted by problems posed by the language, a visit to one of the baths is certainly recommended. They vary greatly – locals tend to use the cheaper ones, tourists may prefer something like the beautiful Gellért baths (worth a visit for the internal decor even if you don't take the waters). There

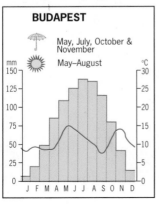

BUDAPEST

May, July, October & November

May–August

mm
150
125
100
75
50
25
0

°C
30
25
20
15
10
5
0

J F M A M J J A S O N D

are all sorts of specialist treatments – cardiac, kidney, gynaecological etc – but the basics are a sauna (*szauna*), followed by a vigorous massage (*masszázs*), then a soak in the hot pool (*gőzfürdő*), which is where the locals tend to spend hours just sitting and chatting. These are all segregated, so make sure you know the words for 'men' (*férfi*) and 'women' (*női*). You will have to throw away all inhibitions, as everyone wanders around completely naked or, at most, in a little apron provided by the establishment, and the attendants and masseuses tend to be somewhat joyless and unsmiling. After the hot pool,

City Park: all the fun of the fair

return to your locker to find your swimsuit and the communal pool for a swim.

CHILDREN

Very young children are not particularly well catered for in Budapest. Only the largest hotels offer a baby-sitting service, cots, highchairs etc. However, baby food, disposable nappies and other basics are available in most supermarkets.

The situation is better where older children are concerned. Young people up to 14 years old are eligible for reductions on all public transport and at campsites.

Boating and cab rides: in summer, boats can be hired on the lake in City Park. For a more

CHILDREN

expensive treat, why not try a
boat trip along the Danube or a
ride in a horse-drawn cab
(*fiacre*) in Buda?

City Park (Városliget): within its
confines you will find a Zoo
(Állatkert), open from 09.00 to
18.00 hrs (16.00 in winter), an
Amusement Park (Vidám Park),
open from 10.00 to 20.00 hrs,
and a spectacular Circus
(Nagycirkusz) with human and
animal acts (Performances:
Wednesday, Thursday, Friday
15.00 and 19.00 hrs, Saturday
and Sunday 10.00 and 15.00 hrs.
Closed Monday, Tuesday).
The **Közlekedési Múzeum**
(Transport Museum) too can be
recommended.

Picnics and playgrounds: if the
weather is hot, you may want to
go for a picnic. There are seats,
as well as open spaces, in the
City Park, on Margaret Island in
the children's playground,
Szabadság tér, and in Jubileum
Park on the slopes of Gellért Hill.

Theatre for children: children
will enjoy a performance by the
colourful marionettes of the State
Puppet Theatre (Állami
Bábszinház), Andrássy út 69, or
the laser theatre shows to the
sound of pop and classical music
at the Planetárium, Metro:
Népliget. For performance
details, check with Tourinform.

**Waxworks (Budavári
Panoptikum)**: the waxworks in
the caves beneath Castle Hill
(entrance in Úri utca 9)
concentrate on the more
gruesome and scandalous
episodes in Hungary's history
and is not for the squeamish
(*Open:* Wednesday to Monday,
10.00 to 18.00 hrs).

Budai-hegység (The Buda

Hills): a little further afield, offer
a pleasant break from the noise
and fumes of the city. Take the
Cogwheel Railway
(Fogaskereku Yasút) from
Szilágyi Erzsébet fasor to
Széchény-hegy. From here you
can ride on the narow-gauge
Children's Railway
(Gyermekvasút) which features
children as ticket collectors and

Dolls in traditional folk costume

station masters. Alternatively, the No. 22 bus from Moszkva tér will take you to the **Game Reserve** (**Vadaspark**). Alight at the Fodor Szanatórium stop. There is a marked nature trail here of about three miles (5km) (*Open:* daily 09.00 to 17.00 hrs).
The Lake Balaton resorts organise children's events. Ask at the tourist offices there.

TIGHT BUDGET

Transport
Public transport is very cheap and efficient and can be recommended as the most cost-effective way to see Hungary. Hitch-hiking is legal except on motorways and is becoming

more common. Cycling is prohibited on motorways and on major roads (those with single digit numbers), effectively cutting out most routes into Budapest. However, bikes may be taken on to trains and some stations even hire them out. For further information contact MÁV (Hungarian State Railways), Andrássy út 35, Budapest VI (tel: 122-7860). The office of the Hungarian Cycling Federation is at Millenáris Sporttelep, Szabó János utca 3, Budapest XIV (tel: 262-0879). They will assist with route planning. Maps can also be obtained from the MCCC (Hungarian Camping and Caravaning Club), Üllői út 6, Budapest VIII (tel: 133-6536).

Accommodation

Most of the tourist offices will arrange private accommodation, either when you get to Budapest or prior to leaving. This kind of accommodation can be a real money saver (although if you're on your own you will almost certainly have to pay for a double room). The tourist offices vet the hosts and the premises but it would be wise to do some research on the location you would like to stay in and ask for a place here. The bonus of this type of accommodation is clearly the chance to see the 'real' Budapest and meet the Pestians. It is worth trying to speak a little Hungarian to break the ice. You will normally be given the keys to the apartment and may come and go as you please.
• If you don't book through a tourist office you can go to your chosen location and look for signs saying *Zimmer Frei* outside

houses and apartments; this indicates bed and breakfast type accommodation is available.
• If there is a group of you it is worthwhile enquiring about apartments to rent; do this through your local tourist agency before you leave for Hungary. Recommended cheaper hotels in the centre of Budapest include:
Citadella, Citadella Sétany, Budapest XI, (tel: 166-5794)
Kulturinnov I, Szentháromság tér 6 (tel: 155-0122)

SPECIAL EVENTS

The following list covers just a few highlights. For further guidance, see the monthly *Programme in Hungary* or *Budapest Panorama*.

February: Film festival. Carnival.

March: Budapest Spring Festival. Ten days of music of all kinds plus plays, ballet, children's events, exhibitions etc. (Events also held in Szentendre).

1 May: Old-style Communist celebrations have now been abolished but the holiday is

Street vendors plying their trade on one of the tourist beats

likely to remain .
Budapest International Fair (concerts, folklore programmes).

Final week of May— book fair. Swimming season, Lake Balaton, begins with a regatta.

20 August: Constitution Day. Firework display on Gellérthegy.

Late September to October: Budapest Autumn Festival (Arts and Music Weeks). Concerts, theatre, ballet, film performances, art exhibitions.

SPORT

For details of sporting fixtures see *Programme in Hungary* or *Budapest Panorama*.

Angling

Fishing permits are issued from regional tourist offices or from hotel reception. A permit valid for the entire country can be obtained from MOHOSZ (Hungarian Fishing Association), Október 6 utca 20, Budapest V (tel: 132-5315).

Football

The national team plays at the Népstadion (Metro line 2). The most popular club sides are Ferencváros, and Kispest Honved. League matches are usually on Saturdays, occasionally on Sundays and Wednesday evenings. No games are played in January.

Horse Racing

Trotting races are held at Kerepesi út, Budapest VIII (meetings on Wednesday at 16.00 hrs and Saturday at 14.00 hrs). Flat racing, recently reintroduced, takes place at Albertirsai út, Budapest X (Metro Örs vezér tere, then bus 100). Thursday at 16.00 hrs and Sunday at 13.30 hrs.

Horse Riding

Whether you want a short ride or a week-long trek there are plenty of opportunities in the countryside around Budapest. Ask IBUSZ for details. Pegazus Tours, Ferenciek tere, Budapest V (tel: 117-1562) also has information on tours, stables and accommodation.

Skating

The artificial lake in the City Park is frozen over for skating in winter.

Swimming

Not all thermal baths have swimming pools attached. However the pools at the Géllert Hotel baths and the Széchenyi baths are some of the most beautiful in Europe. The other places to enjoy a swim are the Palatinus Strand baths on Margaret Island and the Római Fürdő pool at the camping site of the same name (see page 109). For a list of baths and opening times, see page 114.

Lake Balaton has a great many free beaches with swimming areas marked by buoys, also swimming pools. There are still very few nudist beaches in Hungary. For details you should contact Naturisták Szövetsége, Csap utca 3, Budapest I (tel: 115-4863).

Tennis

Courts available at: Flamenco, Bartók Béla út 63, Budapest XI (tel: 166-5699). Várostető Tennis Center, Ózike utca 28, Budapest XIII.

Water Sports

Motor boats are banned on Lake Balaton which makes it ideal for windsurfing. Lake Balaton, some 62 miles (100km) southwest of Budapest, is the largest lake in Central and Western Europe and can be reached from Budapest by the M7 motorway or by train, from the Southern Railway Station, to all the major places on its shores. Equipment can be hired from campsites and the major beaches.

For sailing boats, contact Balatontourist Veszprém, Münnich Ferenc tér 3.

DIRECTORY

Contents

Arriving
Camping
Crime
Customs Regulations
Disabled People
Driving
Electricity
Embassies and
Consulates
Emergency
Telephone
Numbers

Entertainment
Information
Health Regulations
Holidays
Lost Property
Media
Money Matters
Opening Times
Personal Safety
Pharmacies
Places of Worship
Police

Post Office
Public Transport
Senior Citizens
Student and
Youth Travel
Telephones
Time
Tipping
Toilets
Tourist Offices
Travel Agencies

Dramatically sited on the Danube, Visegrád is just two hours away

DIRECTORY

Arriving

To enter Hungary you need a passport valid for at least six months. Visas are no longer required for citizens of the United Kingdom, the United States of America or Canada. Australian citizens should apply for a visa from the following address: Hungarian Consulate, Suite 405, Edgecliff Centre 203–233, New South Head Road, Edgecliff, Sydney, NSW 2027, (tel: (02) 328 7859). Visas (single, multiple entry and transit) can also be obtained at road border crossings and at airports but not at rail crossings. Independent visitors staying more than one month must register at a police station within 48 hours of arrival. Registration is automatic for guests at hotels, motels, campsites etc. Keep your travel documents with you at all times; report any loss to your embassy who will provide you with an exit permit and certificate which you must take to your embassy or consulate. The national carrier is MALÉV Airlines. There are offices at the following addresses:
10 Vigo Street, London W1X 1AJ (tel: (071) 439 0577)
Rockefeller Center, Suite 1900, 630 Fifth Avenue, New York 10111 (tel: 212 757 6480)
175 Bloor Street East, Suite 172, Toronto, Canada (tel: 416 944 0093)

By air

There are scheduled daily flights to Hungary from all European capitals and other major cities, operated by MALÉV and other national airlines. There are normally two flights per day between London and Budapest (flying time 2hrs 10mins) operated by MALÉV and British Airways. MALÉV offer a weekly airbus service direct from New York to Budapest. KLM (Royal Dutch Airlines) also flies from Manchester to Budapest, via Amsterdam. Try the following for cheaper flights/special deals in the UK: Hungarian Air Tours, Kent House, 87 Regent Street, London W1R 7HF (tel: (0171) 437 9405); Danube Travel, 6 Conduit Street, London W1R 9TG (tel: (0171) 493 0263). In the US: Hungarian Travel Bureau, Suite 1104, One Parker Plaza, Fort Lee, New York 07024 (tel: (201) 592 8585).

Budapest Ferihegy airport is situated about 12 miles (20km) southeast of the city centre and has two terminals. MALÉV, Lufthansa, Air France and TWA flights land at the more modern Terminal 2. Other foreign airlines land at Terminal 1. Passport formalities are generally completed in a few minutes and the standard red/green channels are in operation for customs. The usual services such as currency exchange, hotel service, car rental and duty free are available. An airport bus (LRI) operates from both terminals to Erzsébet tér from 06.00 to 22.00 hrs and takes about 40 minutes. Buy your ticket on board. There is also a special shuttle bus which runs between the airport and many of the city's major hotels at a very reasonable cost. Look out for the prominent 'LRI Airport Minibus' sign in the arrivals hall. Taxis are also on hand outside the airport terminal (though notoriously expensive). All taxis should have meters but

On the Danube

agree the approximate fare beforehand.

By train

Only economical if you are under 26; otherwise the cost exceeds either air or coach travel. (For under 26s see **Student and Youth Travel** below.) There is a daily connection to Budapest from London Victoria which makes the journey in approximately 28 hours via Dover, Ostend and Vienna. Alternatively you can change in Paris and travel on the *Orient Express* (this is not incidentally, the glamorous one). All seats, sleepers or couchettes need to be booked well in advance.

If you are already in Eastern Europe there are regular services to Budapest from Vienna and Prague which connect with a number of other centres. During the summer, Saxonia Express operates a road-rail service between Dresden and Budapest carrying private cars and trailers. NB Tourists who do need a visa, should remember that they cannot get one at the border when arriving by train.

By boat

A reasonably priced hydrofoil service operates between Vienna and Budapest from April to October. The journey takes about five hours. The International Boat Station (MAHART) is at Belgrád rakpart. Reserve your seats here (tel: 118-1953) or through any IBUSZ office. Alternatively, seats may be reserved in Vienna at the IBUSZ office at Kartnerstrasse 26, Wien 1 (tel: 53-2686). Visitors may also enter by private boat, providing of course they hold a valid passport and visa where necessary.

By bus

Regular bus services operate from Austria to various

DIRECTORY

destinations in Hungary, including Budapest and Lake Balaton. An alternative route during the summer is via Munich in Germany. International buses arrive at Erzsébet tér (Engels tér).

A smile never needs translation

By car
You can enter Hungary from approximately 30 crossing points in Austria, Slovenia, Croatia, Yugoslavia, Romania, Ukraine and Slovakia. The main Vienna–Budapest road (E60) crosses the Hungarian border at Hegyeshalom.

Camping

There are plenty of campsites in Hungary, many around Lake Balaton (approximately 62 miles (100km) southwest of Budapest). They are open between May and September and are graded to international standards. A basic camp includes running water, toilets, first aid facilities, and stoves for cooking. The more elaborate include restaurants, shops, even discos. Most campsites offer reduced rates for children aged 2–14 and some sites have reductions for members of the International Camping and Caravanning Club. Bungalows can also be found on the major campsites. They sleep 2–4 people and are good value for families.

Information about campsites and their facilities can be obtained from: The Hungarian Camping and Caravanning Club (Magyar Camping és Caravanning Club), Üllői út 6, Budapest VIII (tel: 133-6536)

Camping sites in the Budapest area (selection)

Expo Autocamp, X (part of the fair and exhibition area), Albertirasai út 10 (Gate 4), Budapest X, 500 places for tourists, open mid-June–mid-September.

Caraván, Konkoly-Thege u18b, open April–October.

Hárs-hegy, Hars-hegy, út 7, Budapest II (northwest edge of the city), 480 places, open Easter–October.

Metro-Tenis, Csömöri út 158, Budapest XVI (in eastern part of the city), 50 places, open: April–October.

Mini, Királyok utja 307, Budapest III (in north), 40 places, open: May–September.

Római fürdő, Szentendrei út 189, Budapest III (northern edge of the city), 2,500 places, open all the year round.

Tündérhegy, Szilassy út 8, Budapest XII (Buda Hills), Szilassy u8, 20 places, open all the year round.

Zugligeti, Zugligeti út 101, Budapest XII (near the chairlift at Széchenyi hegy, Buda Hills), 250 places, open March–mid November.

Camping site in Esztergom

Vadvirág Kemping, Báhomi-dű lő, 500 places, open April–September

Camping site in Szentendre

Pap-sziget, Pap-sziget, 200 places, open May–September.

Camping site in Lake Velence

Panoráma, Kemping u2, 2,400 places, open mid-April–mid-October.

Camping sites by Lake Balaton

Kristof Kemping, Véghely u8, Balatonalmádi, 100 places, open April–mid October.

Mini Kemping, Szent László u74, Siófok, 60 places, open May–September.

Chemist (See Pharmacies)

Crime

As in many other Eastern European countries there has been an increase in pick-pocketing and purse snatching, especially in busy shopping streets, on the Metro and other tourist areas. Take basic precautions to protect your property, such as locking your car, storing valuables in the hotel safe etc. Report any serious loss

DIRECTORY

(documents etc) to your embassy immediately. Otherwise contact any IBUSZ representative. The Central Police Station has a thefts office at Deák Ferenc tér 16–18, Budapest V, but there is no guarantee that you will find an English speaker.

Customs Regulations

Because of recent changes in the political situation, these are subject to change. For the latest regulations, consult a Hungarian Consulate or tourist office. The following can be taken into Hungary duty free: 2 litres of wine, 1 litre of spirits, 250 cigarettes or 50 cigars or 250 grammes of tobacco and small presents up to a total value of approximately 8,000 forints. You are allowed to take only a maximum of 1,000 forints per person into Hungary but there is no limit on Western currency. A special permit is required for a hunting rifle and for sophisticated electronic equipment.

You may not bring in: pornography of any kind, narcotics, explosives, firearms and ammunition, pure alcohol. The authorities have now relaxed their interpretation of what constitutes subversive literature, but don't push your luck!

The following can be taken out duty free: 1 litre of spirits (no limit on wine), 400 cigarettes or 50 cigars or 200 grammes of tobacco and small gifts. Everything else is subject to duty. You may not enter or leave the country with surplus petrol or other fuel. A certificate is required to take plants and

animals out of the country. There are certain items that you are not allowed to take out without a permit. For further guidance contact the Customs Office at the Eastern (Keleti) Railway Station, Baross tér, Budapest VIII (tel: 114-0203, 114-0280). See also **Money Matters**.

Disabled People

At present there is little special provision in Hungary for the disabled, but visitors can contact the following for advice and information:

National Federation of the Association of Disabled People, 1032 Budapest, San Marco utca 76, Hungary (tel: 188-8951).

Hungarian Society for the Rehabilitation of Disabled Persons, PO Box 1, H 1528, Budapest 123, Hungary 1. Before you leave Britain contact the Holiday Care Service (tel: 0293 774 535) who are experts in the field of holidays for disabled people.

All of Budapest's 5-star hotels, around half of its 4-star hotels and a few 3- and 2-star claim to be accessible to wheelchair users.

Public places are generally rather poor as regards wheelchair access.

Driving

To drive in Hungary, a valid national driving licence is sufficient, but registration documents and proof of third-party insurance should also be taken.

Main roads in Hungary are generally good and signs follow the standard Continental system. Tickets for motorways, valid for three months, can be bought at

Public transport is cheap and good

border crossing points. Traffic drives on the right and trams always have the right of way. In Budapest itself, driving is as difficult as in any European capital and parking can be a nightmare, with parking spaces in short supply. The public transport system is highly recommended here.

Accidents Report all accidents to the police immediately (tel: 07).
Breakdown assistance Contact the Hungarian Automobile Association (affiliated to the AA): Rómerflóris u4/a Budapest II (tel: 115-2040, for round the clock emergency service tel: 252-8000). Hungarian AA Information Centre with foreign language service, 08.00–16.30 hrs Monday to Friday (tel: 135-3101).

Or contact ÚTINFORM (Highway Information Centre) Dob u75, Budapest VII, (tel: 122-7052). Insurance claims should be made immediately: Hungária Biztosító (Hungarian Insurance Company), Gvadányi utca 69, Budapest XIV (tel: 252-6333).

Car hire Available in Budapest and some larger towns. You will be expected to pay in hard currency. The choice of cars is not as wide as in the West and automatic gearboxes are rare. The driver must be 21 or over and have been in possession of a driving licence for at least a year. The hire price includes comprehensive insurance cover and motor oil.

Avis: via IBUSZ, Szervita tér 8, Budapest V (tel: 118-6222), and at Ferihegy Terminal 1 (tel: 147-5754), Terminal 2 (tel: 157-8470).

Budget: Buda Penta Hotel, Krisztina körút 41–3, Budapest I (tel: 156-6333), and at Ferihegy Terminal 1 (tel: 167-9123), Terminal 2 (tel: 157-8481).

Europcar: Üllői út 60–2, Budapest VIII (tel: 113-1492); Ferihegy Terminal 1 (tel: 157-6680), Terminal 2 (tel: 157-6610).

Hertz: Aranykéz u 4–8, Budapest V (tel: 117-7533), and at Ferihegy Terminal 1 (tel: 157-8618), Terminal 2 (tel: 157-8606).

Fuel ÁFOR petrol stations can be found along most roads. Also, around Budapest there are AGIP, BP, MOL and Shell stations (which also sell Western-made accessories). Self-service is the norm and most garages have lead-free petrol.

Legal requirements Safety belts must be worn in the front seats (and rear seats where fitted) and children under twelve must sit in the back. All vehicles must drive with dipped headlights outside built-up areas in daylight hours. Horns should not be sounded in built-up areas. Motor cyclists must wear helmets. You must carry a spare set of bulbs, a first-aid kit and a red, warning triangle to display in case of breakdown. There is a *total alcohol ban* and visitors are prosecuted with the same severity as residents.

Speed limit 120kmh (74mph) on motorways (80kmh (49mph) for motorbikes), 100kmh (62mph) on highways (70kmh (43mph) for motorbikes), 80kmh (49mph) on main roads and 50kmh (31mph) in built-up areas (same for motorbikes).

Electricity

The electricity supply in Hungary is at the standard 220 volts, 50 cycles AC. Continental-type round two-pin plugs are used. Take a Continental adaptor for 13-amp, square-pin plugs.

Embassies and Consulates

In Budapest

Australia, Délibáb utca 30, Budapest VI (tel: 153-4233)
Canada, Budakeszi út 32, Budapest XII (tel: 176-7711)
Great Britain, Harmincad utca 6, Budapest V (tel: 266-2888)
US, Szabadság tér 12, Budapest V (tel: 112-6450)

Folk costumes vary, but are always colourful – and worn with pride

Hungarian Embassies and Consulates Abroad

Australia Hungarian Consulate, Unit 6, 351a Edgecliff Road, NSW 2027, Sydney (tel: (02) 328-7859)
Canada Hungarian Embassy, 7 Delaware Avenue, Ottowa K2P OZ2, Ontario (tel: (1613) 232-1549)
Great Britain Hungarian Consultate, 35B Eaton Place SW1 (tel: (071) 235-2664)
US Main Consulate, 8 East 75th Street, New York NY 10021 (tel: (212) 879-4127)

Emergency Telephone Numbers

Ambulance 04
Fire 05
Police 07

Entertainment Information

Tourist information offices will have *Programme in Hungary*, a monthly free publication, listing all major concerts from classical to rock. Other English-language listings publications include: *Budapest Panorama* and *Where Budapest* (free magazines) available from information offices and hotel desks; the *Budapest Sun* and *Budapest Week* (newspapers) and *Grapevine* magazine, all available from news-stands. Look out for wall-posters advertising events too. Theatre tickets can be obtained from: the Central Theatre Booking Office (Színházak Központi Jegyirodája), Andrássy út 18, Budapest VI (tel: 1120-000). *Open*: Monday to Friday 10.00–14.00 hrs and 14.30–19.00 hrs.

Entry Formalities See Arriving

Health Regulations

No vaccinations are necessary. The tap water is safe to drink. All

DIRECTORY

visitors to Hungary receive free first aid and transport to hospital. However, there is a charge for all other treatment, so it is essential to take out good health insurance. UK residents are entitled to receive free emergency treatment (UK passport needed). Dental treatment and prescribed medicines must be paid for.

Health Care

Most private clinics have at least one English-speaking doctor; many speak German.

For a 24-hour emergency medical service tel: 118-8288 or 118-8012. For an ambulance tel: 04.

Emergency dental treatment is available at the **Institute of Stomatology**, Mária utca 52, Budapest VIII (tel: 133-0189). Simple medicines such as headache remedies are available without prescription but most other types of medicine require one; if you use contact lenses take any supplies of fluid, etc, with you, as these are scarce in Budapest.

Spa Baths

Hungary has the richest mineral springs in Europe. In Budapest alone, 128 thermal springs service 47 thermal baths, of which 12 are officially recognised as spas. People with heart problems or high blood pressure should take medical advice before undertaking treatment in hot springs. (The Balatonfüred at Lake Balaton is recommended for those with heart disease because the water contains carbonic acid.) A selection of Budapest spas is listed below.

Gellért, Kelenhegyi utca 2–4,

Budapest XI. Various baths, a sauna, solarium and gym etc. The radioactive waters here can cure muscular, nervous and heart diseases.
Open: Monday to Friday 06.30–19.00 hrs; to 13.00 hrs Saturday and to noon on Sunday; wave bath (open air) and other treatments daily 06.00–18.00 hrs.

Király Fürdő Fő utca 84, Budapest II. Original 16th-century Turkish pool with modern facilities. Open alternate days for men and women. Institute for Balneotherapy here offers treatment for rheumatism and arthritis.
Open: Monday to Saturday 06.30–18.00 hrs

Rác Fürdő Hadnagy utca 8–10, Budapest I. Spring water at 40°C (104°F) is good for the skin and for nervous disorders. Original Turkish octagonal pool with dome. Open alternate days for men and women.
Open: Monday to Saturday 06.30–18.00 hrs

Rudas Fürdő Döbrentei tér 9, Budapest I. Built by Ali and Sokoli Mustapha, 16th-century Pashas of Buda. Recommended for kidney stones and stomach problems. Men only.
Open: Monday to Friday 06-30–19.00 hrs, to 13.00 hrs on Saturday and to noon on Sunday wave bath Monday to Saturday 06.00–17.00 hrs, Sunday until noon.

Széchenyi Spa, Vidám Park, Állatkerti körút 11, Budapest XIV Water at 26°C (76°F) effective for rheumatism and neuralgia.
Open: Monday to Friday 06.30–19.00 hrs, Saturday to 13.00 hrs, Sunday to noon; open air pools daily 06.00–18.00 hrs.

The private **Pető Institute**, Kútvölgyi út 6, Budapest XII is world-famous for its treatment of children with spina bifida, cerebral palsy and multiple sclerosis.

Holidays – Public and Religious
New Year's Day
15 March (Anniversary of 1848 Revolution)
Easter Monday
1 May (Labour Day)
20 August (St Stephen's Day)
23 October (Anniversary of 1956 Revolution)
Christmas Day
Boxing Day

Lost Property
On public transport BKV, Akácfa utca 18, Budapest VII (tel: 122-6613)
Open: Monday and Thursday 07.30–15.00 hrs, Wednesday 07.30–19.00 hrs, Friday 07.30–14.00 hrs
For items left on trains try also the information offices at the terminus stations.
For items left on boats contact MAHART, Belgrád rakpart Boat Station, Budapest V (tel: 118–1953).

Media
Some Western newspapers and magazines are available at the central news-stands and in the hotels.
The *Hungarian Times*, the *Daily News*, the *Budapest Sun* and *Budapest Week* are all English-language newspapers published weekly.
English-news magazines are transmitted daily by Radio Bridge (102.1FM) – "Day and Night" – at 8am and 8pm and by Radio Budapest (61.1, 72.2, 93.85 and 1199.1 FM) each night at 11pm. The Hungarian Television station MTV1 has a BBC news

Oblivious to the piece of history commemorated in the plaque, this resident enjoys today's news

bulletin around midnight (times vary, see one of the above newspapers for details). Satellite TV is standard in nearly all 4- and 5-star hotels.

Money Matters

The unit of currency in Hungary is the forint. 1 forint = 100 fillérs (you will not come across this smaller unit often). A maximum of 1,000 forints can be taken in or out of the country. When leaving the country you are only allowed to reconvert currency (from forints to your own money) up to a maximum of 50 per cent of the value of all your money-changing transactions. You will need to prove this, so hang onto your receipts. In any case you may not take out (or bring in) more than 1,000 forints. A single official exchange rate for the forints set daily by the Hungarian National Bank. Money can be exchanged at any of the following: banks, Posta Bank, National Savings Bank (OTP), travel agencies, hotels, most campsites, railway stations, boat piers, airports and some border posts. Travellers' cheques and, sometimes, Eurocheques are acceptable as well as cash. Take your passport for identification. It is inevitable that some time during your stay in Hungary you will be approached by individuals offering to change money on the black market. This practice is illegal and you are advised to ignore any such offers, no matter how tempting, especially as rubbish paper is often wedged between real notes. International credit cards can be used instead of cash in some large restaurants, hotels,

travel agencies and shops. In dire emergencies only, contact your embassy or consulate. Lost travellers' cheques should be reported immediately to the IBUSZ Bank, Ajtósi Dürer sor 10, Budapest XIV (tel: 252-0333).

Opening Times

Banks Monday to Friday 09.00–14.00 hrs
Food shops Monday to Friday 07.00 or 08.00 to 18.00 hrs, Saturday 09.00 or 10.00–13.00 hrs or 14.00 hrs
Museums Generally, Tuesday to Sunday 10.00–18.00 hrs. Times, however, will vary, especially in the smaller museums. Check at your hotel information desk.
Offices Generally Monday to Friday 08.00–16.00 hrs
Post Offices Monday to Friday 08.00–18.00 hrs, Saturday 08.00–12.00 hrs. There are two 24-hour/seven-day post offices in Budapest: at Teréz körút (next to the Western Railway Station) 105 and Baross tér (next to the Eastern Railway Station).
Stores Monday to Friday 10.00–17.00 or 18.00 hrs, (Thursday till 20.00 hrs), Saturday 09.00 or 10.00–13.00 or 14.00 hrs.

Personal Safety

Theft is on the increase in Hungary as tourism expands, so watch your wallet or purse, especially in crowds. As in any city, women may suffer sexual harassment when travelling alone, although Budapest is certainly not among the worst European cities in this respect. Avoid travelling on the 'black train' which leaves Budapest on Friday nights for Debrecen – it is

Village Museum church, Szentendre

notorious for carrying drunken, brawling migrant workers and is not pleasant!
Dial 07 for police, 41 for emergencies.

Pharmacies (*Gyógyszertár* or *Patika*)
Open: Monday to Friday 08.00-20.00 hrs, Saturdays 08.00-14.00 hrs.
Illuminated signs in the windows give addresses of the nearest 24 hr pharmacies.
Pharmacies issue a wide range of drugs, but mostly of East European origin. If, therefore, you require special medication, take it with you. In all pharmacies, you will be expected to place your order, then pay at the cash till before returning to the counter to collect your items.

24-hour seven-day pharmacies in Budapest:

Alkotás utca 1b, Budapest XII (tel: 155-4691)
Rákóczi út 86, Budapest VII (tel: 122-9613)
Széna tér 1, Budapest I (tel: 202-1582)
Teréz körút 41, Budapest VI (tel: 111-4439)

Places of Worship
The majority of Hungarians are Roman Catholics but there are also Protestant, Eastern Orthodox and Jewish minorities. Most large churches are open throughout the day but the smaller ones usually open only at service times.
Visitors are expected to wear modest dress and to refrain from sightseeing while services are in progress.
Mass is held in Hungarian at the Mátyás-templom (Matthias Church) in Buda. Jewish Great Synagogue, Dohány utca 2, Budapest VIII: there are services on Fridays at 18.00 hrs and Saturdays at 09.00 hrs.

Church services in English:
Jesus Heart Jesuit Church, Mária utca 25, Budapest VIII (Saturdays 17.00 hrs).
International Church of Budapest, Óbudai Társáskör (Óbuda Community Centre), Kiskorona utca 7, Budapest III (Sundays 10.30 hrs).
International Baptist Lay Academy, Tapolcsányi utca 7, Budapest II (Sundays 10.30 hrs).
Anglican/Episcopal Church, Vörösmarty utca 51, Budapest VI (1st and 3rd Sunday at 11.00 hrs; 2nd, 4th and 5th Sunday at 09.00 hrs).
Church of Scotland, Vörösmarty utca 51, Budapest VI (2nd and 4th Sunday at 11.00 hrs).

Police
Most police officers have a smattering of German but no other languages. However, they have a good reputation for being helpful to tourists. Their uniforms are blue and grey. Traffic police

The Basilica, Esztergom

are distinguished by white caps and white leather accessories. Police cars are blue and white. The central Police Station in Budapest is at Deák Ferenc u16–18, Budapest V (tel: 118-0800). Advice for foreign tourists tel: 111-8668.

Post Office

Open: Monday to Friday 08.00–18.00 hrs, Saturday 08.00–12.00 hrs.

There are 24-hour, seven-day post offices near the Western and Eastern Railway Stations (Teréz körút 105 and Baross tér 11c respectively). Poste restante mail can be collected from the post office at Városház utca 18. Remember that Hungarians put surnames first so your letters may be filed under your first name initial by mistake. Stamps can also be bought at tobacconists (*bélyeg*) and in hotels. Post boxes, which are emptied daily, are red and decorated with a hunting horn. For telegrams, dial 02 (occasionally an English-speaking operator can be found) or call at a main post office. Fax machines can be found in most hotels and at the Central Post Office at Petőfi Sándor utca 13–19, Budapest V.

Public Transport

Boats Boat services operate along the Danube and on Lake Balaton from April to late September. The MAHART service between Budapest and the towns on the Danube bend leaves from Vigadó tér boat station (tel: 118-1223). Vienna can be reached by a hydrofoil service which leaves from the International Boat Station on Belgrád rakpart (from April to October). For reservations contact an IBUSZ office or MAHART, Belgrád rakpart (tel: 118-1953).

Buses (Say 'booss' for bus, not 'bus', which is extremely rude in Hungarian!) Buses are cheap but crowded, especially at rush hours. Timetables are available at the main bus terminal, Erzsébet tér, but in the heavy city trafic don't rely on the schedules. There are some night buses, but most services end at 23.00 hrs. Bus stops display a blue-bordered bus symbol and the letter 'M': there is usually a route map and a list of stops. Yellow bus tickets (which must be purchased in advance) can be bought from machines, metro stations and tobacco shops – one ticket per ride. They should be validated as you board. Bus and tram tickets are not interchangeable but passes are available.

Long distance buses run to other towns and resorts. Seats must be booked in advance. For further information contact Erzésbet tér Bus Station.

International services operate to Vienna and Munich.

Metro Budapest's underground system was the first to be built on mainland Europe and was opened in 1896 for the millennial celebrations. There are three lines (blue No. 3, red No. 2 and yellow No.1) intersecting at Deák tér. The system is fast, clean and safe. Routes are clearly indicated and all stations display maps. Trains operate from 05.00 to 23.00 hrs, so beware of missing last connections! There is a flat

fare for each journey. Buy a
yellow ticket from the machine in
the entrance or from the ticket
window, then punch it in the
machine as you approach the
escalator. (On the yellow line,
the tickets have to be punched
on the train). A new ticket is
needed if you change lines.
Taxis Budapest taxis are usually
cheap and plentiful. All cabs are
fitted with meters and charges
are usually displayed. Pay only
in forints but add a 10 per cent
tip. Cabs may be hired from a
stand, hailed, or ordered by
phone, but do not expect the
drivers to speak a foreign
language. Try to stick to using
the firms listed here. Tel:

Budataxi 120-0200; Citytaxi 153-
3633; Radiotaxi 177-7777.
Trains Hungary has a cheap and
efficient rail network and all the
main provincal towns can be
reached by express train from
Budapest (seat reservations
essential). The HÉV suburban
railway serves Budapest and its
environs. Yellow signs indicate
departures (*induló*), white ones
arrivals (*érkező*). Tickets (also
yellow) may be used for stations
within the city limits. Other
tickets can be bought up to 60
days in advance and various
concessions are available:
children under 4 travel free;
those aged 4–10 travel at half
price and there are reduced

rates for parties and senior citizens. Seven and ten-day excursion tickets are also available. For tickets and information contact MÁV Central Booking Office, Andrássy út 35, Budapest VI. Tel: 142-9150 (international) or 122-7860 (national) for an English language information service during office hours. Most international trains leave from the Eastern Station (Keleti). All international fares must be paid in hard currency.

Trams and trolley-buses
Services operate between 05.00 and 23.00 hrs. (There is a limited night service). Tickets (yellow) are sold at metro stations, tobacconists, kiosks and by vending machines – punch them as you board. You can buy a 24-hour ticket (*napijegy*) which enables you to travel by bus, tram, metro and suburban train (HÉV) anywhere in the city. Three, seven and 14 day passes are also available from main stations (passport-sized photo necessary).

Budapest's Central Market Hall, built in the 1890s

Senior Citizens

Senior citizens with Rail Europe Senior Cards can claim a 33 per cent reduction on train fares.

Student and Youth Travel

An International Union of Students card (the East European equivalent of ISIC) will entitle you to reductions at hostels and campsites, reduced admission to museums, and generous discounts on trains and MALÉV flights. Expressz Központi Iroda, Szabadság tér 16, Budapest V (tel: 131-7777) provides information on all student discounts and opportunities in Hungary. They

Public telephone kiosk

will also help with hostel accommodation. International Student Identity and International Youth Hostel Federation cards can all be bought here but take a plentiful supply of passport-sized photographs with you.

See also **Camping** p. 109 and **Accommodation** pp. 92–3 and 102. There are few facilities for cyclists in Hungary. It is illegal to cycle on motorways and major trunk roads but some stations have bikes for hire.

The Hungarian Cycling Federation Office is at Millenáris Sporttelep, Szabó János utca 3, Budapest XIV.

Telephones

Most phone boxes are green-

and-yellow or white.
For long-distance calls inside
Hungary dial 06, the district
code, then the individual
number.
English language directory
enquiries (07.00–20.00 hrs) tel:
267-7111.
Use the red telephone kiosks to
make international calls. If you
get into difficulties dial the
international operator on 09.
For international calls dial 00,
before the country code, area
code (minus the initial 0) and
number.
Australia 61
Britain 44
Canada 1
New Zealand 64
United States 1
When phoning into Hungary
from abroad, the country code is
36 and the Budapest code is 1.

Time

Central European time, ie one
hour ahead of Britain GMT, six
hours ahead of Canada and the
United States (Eastern
seaboard), eight hours behind
Australia (Sydney), and 11 hours
ahead of New Zealand.

Tipping

Tipping is customary in Hungary.
Porters, maids, cloakroom
attendants, guides, garage
attendants, waiters and of
course, gypsy violinists will all
expect tips of between 50 and
300 forints.
There are no hard and fast rules
but 10–5 per cent is standard for
waiters and taxi drivers. The
custom is to tip at the same time
as paying.

Toilets

There are plenty of public toilets

in Budapest. As elsewhere those
in cafés, restaurants or hotels
tend to be cleaner. Leave a few
forints in the saucer by the door.
Signs *mosdó* or *WC: férfi*–men,
női–women

Tourist Offices

In Hungary
Tourinform, Sütő utca 2,
Budapest (near Deák tér) (tel:
117-9800); open Monday to
Saturday 08.00–20.00 hrs.
Kossuth L utca 28, Keszthely (tel:
83/314-286)
Fő utca 41, Siófok (tel: 84/310-
117)
Dumtsa j utca 22, Szentendre
(tel: 26/317-965).

In Great Britain
Danube Travel, 6 Conduit Street,
London W1R 9TG (tel: (0171)
493-6963)

In United States
IBUSZ One Parker Plaza, Suite
1104, Fort Lee, N.J. 07024 (tel:
201 592 8585)

Travel Agencies

In Hungary
Cityrama, Báthory utca 22,
Budapest V (tel: 132-5344)
IBUSZ, Felszabadulás tér 5,
Budapest V (tel: 137-0939)
IBUSZ Hotel Service, Petőfi tér 3,
Budapest V (tel: 117-9099)
Budapest Tourist, Roosevelt tér
5–7 (tel: 117-3555)
MAHART boat trips, Siótour,
Batthyány utca 2b, Siófok (tel: 84
313 111)
MALÉV Air Tours, Roosevelt tér
2, Budapest V (tel: 118-6614)
MAV Tours, Teréz körút 62,
Budapest VI (tel: 269-1602).
Taverna Tourist Service, Hotel
Taverna, Váci utca 20, Budapest
V (tel: 118-7287).

LANGUAGE

LANGUAGE

Hungarian (Magyar) lies outside the mainstream of European languages. Like Finnish, Estonian and Siberian Chuvash, it belongs to the Finno-Ugric group, so there is little room for guesswork and improvisation. Fortunately, English is spoken at hotel reception desks etc, though German is much more widely understood. Restaurants generally provide menus in the major European languages but, if you are eating out in an *Étterem*, or drinking in an ordinary Hungarian bar, you will have to point or resort to the phrase book. Shopping is less of a problem, at least in the major department stores but if you don't feel confident stick to Váci utca. Try at least to learn the Hungarian words for please, thank you, good day. It is a courtesy that will be appreciated and may win you friends. Hungarian has at least one thing going for it: the pronunciation is very straightforward and each word without exception carries a slight accentuation on the first syllable.

Pronunciation

Vowels
a like English o in not
á like the a in car
e as in yes
é like day
i as in hit
í as in see
o like over
ó as above but longer
ö like the ur in fur
ő as above but longer
u like pull
ú as in rule
ü like the French *un* or German *fünf*
ű as above but longer

Consonants
b, d, f, h, m, n, v, x, z as in English
c like the ts in nets
cs like the ch in chap
g as in go
gy like the d in during
j like the y in yes
ny like ni in onion
p soft as in sip
r trilled like the Scottish
s like sh in ship
sz like s in so
t soft as in sit
zs like the s in pleasure

The Basics

Good day	Jó napot kivánok	**Saturday**	Szerda
Yes	Igen	**Sunday**	Csütörtök
No	Nem	**One**	Egy
Please	Kérem	**Two**	Két
Thank you	Köszönöm	**Three**	Három
OK	Jó	**Four**	Négy
Excuse me	Bocsánat	**Five**	Öt
I'm English/American		**Six**	Hat
Anglo-amerikai vagyok		**Seven**	Hét
Monday	Hétfő	**Eight**	Nyolc
Tuesday	Kedd	**Nine**	Kilenc
Wednesday	Péntek	**Ten**	Tíz
Thursday	Szombat	**Eleven**	Tizenegy
Friday	Vasárnap	**Twelve**	Tizenket

Thirteen	Tisenhárom	**Free admission**	a belépés ingyenes
Twenty	Húsz	**Toilet**	Mosdó or WC
Twenty-one	Huszonegy	(pronounced vai-tsai)	
Thirty	Harminc	**Men**	Férfi
Forty	Negyven	**Women**	Női
Fifty	Ötven	**Hotel**	Szálló or Szálloda
Sixty	Hatvan	**Room to let**	Szoba kiadó
Seventy	Hetven	**No smoking**	Tilos a dohányzás
Eighty	Nyolcvan	**Caution**	Vigyázat
Ninety	Kilencven	**Bus or train stop**	Megálló
One Hundred	Száz	**Tram**	Villamos

Signs

Entrance	Bejárat
Exit	Kijárat
Arrival	Érkezés
Departure	Indulas
Open	Nyitva
Closed	Zárva

Police station	Rendőrség
Airport	Repülőtér

Shopping can be fun especially if you try and learn a few words of Hungarian

Other Useful Phrases

I'd like Szeretnék
Where is/are? Hol van/vannak?
How much is it? Mennyibe kerül?
The bill please Kérem a számlát

INDEX

INDEX/ACKNOWLEDGEMENTS

Acknowledgements

The Automobile Association wishes to thank the following photographers and libraries for their assistance in the preparation of this book.

MARY EVANS PICTURE LIBRARY 6/7 Peasants in battle array, 7 Admiral Horthy

NATURE PHOTOGRAPHERS LTD 79 Red-breasted flycatcher (R Tidman), 81 White stork (P R Sterry), 82 Grt Bustard (K J Carlson).

The remaining photographs were taken by Eric Meacher (© AA Photo Library) with the exception of pages 32/3, 54, 88 and 125 taken by Ken Paterson.

Copy editor for original edition: Sue Gordon
For this revision: Copy editor Jenny Fry; Verifiers; Paul Murphy & Colin Follett
Thanks also to Christopher & Melanie Rice for their help with this revision.